Interview in Weehawken

INTERVIEW IN WEEHAWKEN

The

BURR-HAMILTON DUEL

AS TOLD IN THE

Original Documents

Edited by
HAROLD C. SYRETT AND JEAN G. COOKE
With an Introduction and Conclusion by
WILLARD M. WALLACE

Wesleyan University Press
MIDDLETOWN, CONNECTICUT

973.4
S
c 1

Library of Congress Catalog Card Number: 60–7259
Manufactured in the United States of America
First edition

"I was . . . furnished with a communication demanding a personal interview."

—WILLIAM P. VAN NESS TO NATHANIEL PENDLETON

Contents

Illustrations

Abbreviations

AD   Autograph Document
ADS   Autograph Document Signed
ADf   Autograph Draft
ADfS   Autograph Draft Signed
AL   Autograph Letter
ALS   Autograph Letter Signed
DS   Document Signed
JCH Transcripts   John C. Hamilton Transcripts.
        These transcripts are owned by Mr. William
        Swan, Hampton Bays, New York, who has
        placed them on loan in the Columbia Univer-
        sity Library.

Interview in Weehawken

INTRODUCTION

Introduction

A few minutes after seven o'clock on the bright morning of July 11, 1804, pistols flashed in America's most celebrated duel. The bullet of the challenged, Alexander Hamilton, knocked bark and twigs from a tree limb. That of the challenger, Aaron Burr, penetrated his opponent's right side, inflicting a mortal wound.

This duel, which destroyed the life of one principal and ruined that of the other, was but the climax of a long-standing rivalry. The rivalry manifested itself possibly in their military aspirations but certainly in the law, business, and politics. It was even scurrilous gossip that for a time the two men were suitors for the same mistress. Actually their enduring competition became a kind of minor theme in a more significant story, the power struggle between Hamilton and Thomas Jefferson. At the same time it had a dynamic of its own, which then gave it political importance and which continues to present it as a fascinating study in human relations.

The time of the first meeting of Hamilton and Burr is not known for sure. Both were in Elizabethtown, New Jersey, in 1773, when Hamilton, only recently arrived from the West Indies, was frantically trying to catch up on his education at Francis Barber's grammar school before entering college, and when Burr, having graduated from Princeton, was pursuing an independent course of readings, as well as the young ladies of the town, and considering the choice of a career. If they saw each other at all, which is only a possibility, it is unlikely they had much to do with each other in view of the disparity in their education.

Three years later, with the Revolutionary War on, they could scarcely have avoided at least a nodding acquaintance. Hamilton, after having studied at King's College in New York and having delivered speeches for the Patriot cause, obtained command of a provincial battery of artillery. He was now nineteen years old and a captain.[1]

Burr too had moved rapidly. Following a year of theology in Bethlehem, Connecticut, with a friend of his grandfather Jonathan Edwards, he studied law at Litchfield under his brother-in-law, Tapping Reeve. With the outbreak of war, he presently enrolled as a gentleman volunteer in Arnold's expedition to Quebec — this over the opposition of his uncle, who had been his guardian since he was a child. Burr's gallantry at Quebec ultimately helped gain him a place on General Washington's staff, but, eager for action, he soon obtained a transfer to the staff of General Putnam, commander of the New York garrison. He was now twenty years old and a major.[2]

The disastrous New York campaign of 1776 found Burr and Hamilton actively engaged. When General Howe landed on Staten Island in August, 1776, Washington resolved to hold New York regardless of overwhelming British land and sea power. Accordingly he divided his forces and fortified Brooklyn Heights. Among the troops sent over to the Heights were Hamilton and Burr. Both were critical of Washington's decision; and Howe's landing on Long Island and his defeat of the Americans vindicated their judgment. Only British caution and lethargy and a run of murky weather which permitted Washington to withdraw one night to Manhattan prevented a military catastrophe.

Although Hamilton and Burr may still have been unacquainted except by reputation, Hamilton soon had occasion to notice the other man. On September 15 Howe invaded Manhattan, routed the American army, and cut off a number of units in lower Manhattan. These last included troops under General Henry Knox; and with Knox was Hamilton. Knox was preparing to make a last-ditch stand when Burr galloped up and offered to lead the troops by a little-known road to Harlem Heights and safety. When Knox insisted that retreat was hopeless, Burr appealed to the troops themselves. Although the speech was grossly insubordinate, the men cheered him and followed him into the American lines. It was a close thing, however, and at one point Burr with two mounted companions had to chase away an enemy patrol with the British army less than a mile away. Some of the glitter passed from Knox's Boston reputation, while Hamilton's baggage and one of his guns fell into the hands of the British. Burr's performance received no official mention.[3]

Hamilton soon had his taste of glory too. At the battle of White Plains his battery took an admirable if losing part in the defense of Chatterton Hill. Later, with the New York campaign utterly lost and Washington fleeing across New Jersey, Hamilton in the rear guard handled his guns with professional competence. During the Trenton-Princeton campaign of 1776–1777, when Washington's victories revived the martial spirit of the country, Hamilton played a lively role, particularly at Princeton. The winter finally brought recognition in his promotion to lieutenant colonel and appointment as aide-de-camp to Washington.

Since Putnam's command was charged with the defense of Philadelphia, Burr, to his deep regret, missed the winter campaign. He also resented the promotion over his head of officers junior to him in service. Even when he received an appointment as lieutenant colonel of Colonel William Malcolm's regiment in the summer of 1777, he continued resentful.[4] But whereas Benedict Arnold, experiencing the same treatment, blamed his enemies in the army and Congress, Burr felt that in his case Washington himself was responsible.

If the subsequent war experience of Burr and

Hamilton had flashes of glory, it had also a great deal of discouragement and disillusionment, particularly for Burr. At Valley Forge in the winter of 1777–1778 he supported Generals Horatio Gates and Charles Lee as possible successors to Washington. The following June, during the battle of Monmouth, when Washington tried to halt General Clinton's withdrawal from Philadelphia to New York, Burr, still only a lieutenant colonel, commanded a brigade. He did some extraordinarily effective fighting but at one juncture carried his initiative to the point of disobeying Washington's orders. He never again controlled in action a large body of troops or knew another promotion.

Like Lee, Burr felt victimized by Washington, for whose strategy or tactics he had little respect. The General's deficiencies in these matters Burr never ceased to deplore, while he was bitter over Washington's reluctance to commandeer supplies at Valley Forge until the last. Many of Burr's comments were to the point, but he never perceived Washington's solid virtues.

Although ill as a result of overexertion at Monmouth, Burr soon returned to duty. He served briefly at West Point and then, in the winter of 1779, took charge of the Westchester lines, where he did excellent work in restoring order. In March, however, ill health forced his retirement. He returned only momentarily to action in July, 1779, to lead a number of militia and Yale students against the British, who had invaded New Haven.

Hamilton's efforts were more notable. As one of Washington's amanuenses he contributed to making the commander in chief's correspondence remarkable for its lucidity and facility of expression. He also went on numerous missions. In battle he was ever the prompt, loyal aide, his work at Brandywine and Monmouth being outstanding. After the latter battle he was eager to fight a duel with the disobedient General Lee, but his friend John Laurens challenged first, and Hamilton served as Laurens' second. He also testified against Lee at the latter's court-martial.

By 1780 Hamilton was restless with his assignment and impatient with Washington's cold, precise manner, his "self-love," his lack of "delicacy" and "good temper," and his inflexibility in the case of Major John André. "Our dispositions," said Hamilton, "are the opposite of each other."[5] A brief but sharp altercation occurred early in 1781, followed by an unsatisfactory reconciliation, and Hamilton left the service. He returned, however, in time to command a battalion of light infantry at Yorktown, where he brought off a handsome assault on Cornwallis' entrenchments. Within a month after the British surrender he was off to Albany and the home of General Philip Schuyler, whose daughter Elizabeth he had married the previous year.

Both Hamilton and Burr found wives in the course of the war. Hamilton married his Eliza, as he called her, the second of the three Schuyler daughters, in December, 1780. He had first met her three years earlier. She had a quiet charm, a mild temperament, and an enormous capacity for devotion — hardly a type designed to appeal to the intellectual, energetic Hamilton. Yet he loved her, and despite his subsequent straying he continued to esteem her highly. Nor did Eliza permit anything to interrupt the tide of her devotion. It is not unlikely, of course, that Hamilton also had in mind the political advantages of his marriage, for the Schuylers were a great power in New York State and influential in the Continental Congress. On the other hand, Schuyler liked the young man, was greatly impressed with his ideas on politics and public finance, and welcomed the match with enthusiasm.

If the marriage of the illegitimate, impecunious Hamilton with a member of the patrician Schuyler family was extraordinary, that of Aaron Burr with Theodosia Prevost was almost incredible. In 1777, when Burr first met her at Paramus, New Jersey, Theodosia was the wife of a British colonel on duty in the West Indies. She was also ten years older than Burr and the mother of five children! Although no beauty by any calculation, she was a woman of refinement and grace, and she possessed a love of reading and ideas. To her home, which she shared with her mother and sister, came many American officers for an evening of serious discussion, chaff, and song. She grew to know and to be well liked by officers such as Washington and Lee, James Monroe and Hamilton. And, of course, there was Burr, whose reading in the great French and English writers of the day she tried to guide with discretion. While she was pleased to observe his admiration for Voltaire, it troubled her to see him prefer a scoffer like Chesterfield to Rousseau. Gradually she drew him out of his disillusionment and cynicism. When Burr finally recognized that the nature of his feeling for her was becoming far different from that of a son for a mother or a brother for an older sister, he remained away from her for months until he learned of the death of Colonel Prevost. Even afterward he was so circumspect that friends thought his visits were to see Theodosia's unmarried sister.

But Burr, whose patrimony had been pretty thoroughly exhausted by his war expenses, needed to make a living. Accordingly he started again the study of law. Regulations required three years of preparation before a candidate for the bar could take his examinations. Burr could not wait. He studied six months under competent tutors, then raced to Albany to obtain a time waiver. A bill passed by the New York Legislature disbarring Tory lawyers opened up such promising possibilities that Burr persuaded influential friends to intercede for him. Eventually the Albany bar dispensed with the three-year rule in the case of veterans but insisted on his taking the examination. This obstacle he hurdled with ease and, licensed in January, 1782, began in April to practice in Albany. Less than three months later he married Theodosia Prevost, thus becoming the stepfather of five children at the age of twenty-six.

Hamilton, a veteran too, also passed the bar examination after an equally furious and brief preparation, in the very month that Burr married. He too had his eye on New York City and eagerly awaited the British evacuation. In the meantime he helped Robert Morris by serving briefly as collector of Continental revenues in New York. His chief concern as he looked over the national scene was for a sound public financial policy and a strong central government, and he wrote articles of this purport for public and private distribution. He was also elected to the Continental Congress. While in Congress, he vigorously advocated his dual concern. The experience he acquired in Philadelphia accentuated his aversion to a government in which the real power rested not in Congress but in the states. Eventually, however, bread-and-butter necessity impelled him to resign and avail himself of the lucrative legal opportunities in New York City.

With the British evacuation in November, 1783, Hamilton and Burr, along with a corps of brilliant contemporaries, had all the legal business they could take care of. Hamilton won many substantial clients by reason of his political philosophy and his celebrated if only partially successful defense of a merchant sued under the Trespass Act of New York, by which citizens could receive damages for property occupied and misused by Tories during the war. Hamilton's line of reasoning was that the Trespass Act was contrary to the peace treaty and thereby jeopardized the supremacy of the Articles of Confederation. His belief in a sound financial policy led him to draw up the constitution and charter for the Bank of New York, which was supported by merchants and city property owners. He became a director in this bank. At the same time he successfully opposed the establishment of a land bank in which the great landowner Robert R. Livingston was interested. Respected — and feared — for his political and financial views, eagerly sought after by wealthy clients, and adored by his wife, who eventually bore him eight children, Hamilton was creating a great reputation.

If Hamilton was making money and a name, so was Burr — and so were Robert Troup, Henry Brockholst Livingston, and other brilliant young lawyers. Although the leadership of the bar fell to Hamilton, Burr was generally considered the best courtroom lawyer of the lot. Conversational in manner and voice, not given to long harangues, occasionally employing dramatic tricks of exposure, he was in great demand. Whereas Hamilton, rising "to the loftiest heights of professional eminence," was strong on the principle of the law, solid in organization and detailed evidence, and oratorical in delivery though feeble of voice, Burr was an astute legal tactician, ever — as James Kent said — "acute, quick, terse, polished, sententious, and sometimes sarcastic in his forensic discussions. He seemed to disdain illustration and expansion, and confined himself with stringency to the point in debate."[6] Not infrequently the two men collaborated on a case and formed an unbeatable combination. When opposed to one another, as they sometimes were, Burr, with an almost prescient sense of the weak points in Hamilton's logic, would demolish the effect of the other's extended, careful presentation in a few minutes. An able contemporary, General Erastus Root, also a lawyer, said of the legal abilities of these two luminaries, who were friendly but hardly intimate, "They were much the greatest men in this State, and perhaps the greatest men in the United States."[7]

Meanwhile Burr remained devoted to his wife, carefully directed the studies of his stepchildren, and became passionately attached to his own daughter, who was born in 1783 and whom he insisted on naming after his wife.

However busily occupied with his legal work, Hamilton found his attention turning increasingly to the national crisis occasioned in good part by the deficiencies of the Articles of Confederation as an instrument of national government. His activity in the Annapolis Convention and as one of the representatives in the Constitutional Convention in Philadelphia is a familiar story. Likewise familiar is his role in joining with Madison and Jay to write the Federalist papers, that magnificent polemic designed to convince all men, but particularly the voters of New York State, of the virtues of the Constitution.

Burr engaged in no activity of comparable significance. He held himself independent of both the Federalists and the anti-Federalists. Although he favored the Constitution, he thought it would not last fifty years. For that matter, Hamilton himself thought none too highly of the Constitution; it was too filled with compromises for his taste. His distrust of the people led him to favor giving more power to the rich and well-born. With his eye on the British constitution and social structure, he wanted two checks in order to balance an assembly chosen by the people: a senate of large-propertied men to serve for life and an executive, also to serve for life, who should have veto power over the national and state legislatures. While he regretted that his own plan was unacceptable to the other Founders, he preferred the Constitution as drafted to the weak central government existing under the Articles of Confederation.

The same public spirit evinced in New York during the Constitutional struggle, when his new Federalist forces defeated those of Governor George Clinton over the question of the unconditional acceptance of the Constitution, led Hamilton in September, 1789, to accept the new Cabinet post of Secretary of the Treasury. It would be hard to overestimate the importance of a number of his achievements in this office: assumption by the national government of the states' debts, meeting the interest on the national debt by a tariff on imports and an excise tax on distilled whisky, and the establishment of a national bank chartered by Congress. There have always been critics of these policies, but there can be little doubt that they served at the time to strengthen the public credit. It it also true that they helped split the country into opposing factions, the Federalists drawing their inspiration from Hamilton and the more democratic Republicans looking to Jefferson.

With Hamilton a national figure, his very name an object of admiration or contumely, Burr was operating on a less grandiose scale yet was gradually enlarging his role. In 1788 he stood as an anti-Federalist candidate for the Assembly from New York City. The next year, Hamilton, seeking the overthrow of the Clinton faction by a combination of the Schuyler and Livingston forces, hit upon Judge Robert Yates as a gubernatorial candidate to oppose Clinton and secured the appointment of Burr as one of a committee to support Yates' candidacy. This Federalist alignment on Burr's part was not too remarkable since Yates had assisted him in obtaining admission to the bar. Burr was therefore paying off a personal obligation rather than identifying himself as pro-Hamilton or anti-Clinton. That Clinton, an amazingly successful politician and the son of an immigrant from Ireland, recognized Burr's position was made clear enough after he defeated Yates in a race so close that, although Clinton won the gubernatorial election for the fourth time, both houses of the Legislature were captured by the Federalists. Deciding that he needed new sources of strength, Clinton then offered the attorney generalship to Burr, who accepted in September, 1789.

Up to this point Burr had shown little of Hamilton's enthusiasm for a political life. He had been more interested in his vocation and his family, particularly his daughter and his wife, whose health, he sadly noted, was becoming precarious. From now on, however, politics increasingly claimed his interest. At the same time, he never approached politics with the hot passion of Hamilton or the intense but somewhat colder sentiment of John Adams. Burr persisted in remaining independent of party factionalism, so far as that was possible. While others became rancorous, Burr was cool, detached, reasonable. He followed the developments of the French Revolution with interest and sympathy but with little of the enthusiasm and invincible optimism that characterized Jefferson. If he suspected that the masses — whether French or American — could be brought to an appreciation of their responsibility in government only after a long process of education, he did not share Hamilton's fear and distrust of them. Charmingly courteous to great and humble alike, Burr brought to his political offices a rational efficiency that excited admiration and an objectivity of view that roused suspicion in his factious era that he was primarily serving his own interests. The suspicion was probably well warranted, too, though one cannot be certain of the motivations of this subtle, mysterious person, who preferred, usually with consistency, to keep his own counsel.

As attorney general of New York he was very active. He was eminently successful in settling a variety of disputes emerging from the Revolution, particularly in establishing which claims properly belonged within the purview of the state and which within that of the federal government. Since he was a member of the Land Commission by virtue of his office, his absence from the state in mid–1791 may have saved him from direct involvement in a great land speculation deal in the western and northern counties, but it did not spare him from suspicion of complicity. Furthermore, while in office, he appointed the committee which determined the rerouting of the Boston Post Road. The fact that the new route went through property Burr had recently purchased, thus enabling him to make a tidy profit, seemed more than coincidence.

Burr was presently on his way to higher office. In the first elections for the United States Senate, the Federalists chose General Schuyler and Rufus King, late of Massachusetts. The election of the latter, who had been selected by Hamilton, enraged the Livingstons, who thought that one of their number should have been nominated. Hence, when the short term of Schuyler expired, with the General anticipating re-election, the Livingstons joined the Clinton faction in securing the election of Burr. Schuyler was deeply hurt and Hamilton as deeply angered, and both held Burr to a large degree responsible. In reality it was anti-Hamilton sentiment and Clinton's belief that he could win the independent-minded Burr to his side that were chiefly responsible. But henceforth, although they preserved the social amenities, Hamilton seemed to have seen in Burr a rival who, sooner or later, would have to be eliminated from the political arena.

Actually he was not given too much cause to worry by Burr's performance in the Senate. Burr's part in the introduction or discussion of bills on the Senate floor was minor, although he served on numerous committees and presumably made valuable contributions in this more private medium. He opposed the Jay treaty and a number of Hamilton's financial measures but with little success. He tried in vain to persuade the Senate to permit the public to attend debates. He held out strongly for an adequate army and became interested in foreign policy. He even started a history of the Revolution, which unfortunately came to an abrupt stop when Jefferson, as Secretary of State, suddenly denied him access to the archives. But though Burr attended to his senatorial duties, he was unutterably bored much of the time and took advantage of long speeches by his colleagues to write some instructive and fascinating letters to his young daughter Theodosia. His wife's death from cancer in 1794 dealt him a heavy blow; it was only afterward that he began to live up to his formidable reputation as a gallant.

If Burr's senatorial career gave Hamilton little cause to fear, the same cannot be said of his activities in New York. In the gubernatorial campaign of 1792 there was difficulty finding a Federalist opponent to Clinton, and strong sentiment developed for Burr. Hamilton, however, persuaded John Jay to leave the Supreme Court and become a candidate. Among the Republicans there was marked dissatisfaction with the idea of continuing to support Clinton; hence a large body of New York City Republicans backed Burr. Ultimately the Clinton forces were clearly triumphant in the nomination, but the election was disputed, with

Jay showing a slight majority. To settle the dispute, which involved alleged irregularities in three of the upper counties where Jay had been popular, the two Senators, Burr and King, were called on for legal opinion. When they disagreed, each assembled a distinguished array of legal talent in support. Eventually the Legislature voted in line with Burr's recommendations; and the result was a reinstatement of Clinton as governor for yet another term. As a reward to Burr, but perhaps also to shackle him, Clinton offered his name as a judge of the Supreme Court of New York. Burr politely refused to consider the offer.

Hamilton's exasperation at Burr's role in the gubernatorial campaign turned to sharp anger at his performance in the Presidential campaign of that same year, 1792. The gubernatorial campaign had marked Burr as a Republican, and the Republicans were highly in favor of nominating Jefferson, Clinton, or Burr as vice-president. Washington as the Presidential candidate was to go unchallenged, but Vice-President Adams was regarded as legitimate prey. Burr at once began to muster support for himself in other states. Disturbed, Rufus King reported to Hamilton not only the extent of this activity but also the possibility that Adams' margin might be so close he would resign.

Hamilton quickly reached for pen and ink. To fellow Federalists he sketched the danger in letters that fairly smoked with the intensity of his alarm and of his distrust of Burr. "Mr. Clinton's success I should think very unfortunate," he wrote to one correspondent. "But still Mr. C. is a man of property, and in private life, as far as I know, of probity. I fear the other gentleman [Burr] is unprincipled, both as a public and a private man. When the Constitution was in deliberation, his conduct was equivocal, but its enemies, who, I believe, best understood him, considered him as with them. In fact, I take it, he is for or against nothing, but as it suits his interest or ambition. He is determined, as I conceive, to make his way to be the head of the popular party, and to climb *per fas et nefas* to the highest honors of the State, and as much higher as circumstances permit. Embarrassed, as I understand, in his circumstances, with an extravagant family, bold, enterprising, and intriguing, I am mistaken if it be not his object to play the game of confusion, and I feel it a religious duty to oppose his career."[8]

This was strong language; but, having assured King that good use would be made of his information, Hamilton expressed himself to another gentleman with even greater vehemence and rashness. "Mr. Burr's integrity as an individual is not unimpeached," he said acidly. "As a public man, he is one of the worst sort — a friend to nothing but as it suits his interest and ambition. . . . 'Tis evident that he aims at putting himself at the head of what he calls the 'popular party' as affording the best tools for an ambitious man to work with, secretly turning liberty into ridicule. He knows as well as most men how to make use of the name. In a word, if we have an embryo-Caesar in the United States, 'tis Burr."[9]

Although a fortnight later Hamilton inscribed a letter to Charles Cotesworth Pinckney of South Carolina in somewhat the same vein, mentioning Burr as ambitious for "the full honors of the State" and as "a man in private life not unblemished," he could also write, five days after the Pinckney letter, a much more restrained epistle to John Steele, a congressman from North Carolina. "My opinion of Mr. Burr is yet to form," he said in disregard of sentiments expressed in the previous letters, "but, according to the present state of it, he is a man whose only political principle is to *mount at all events,* to the highest legal honors of the nation, and as much further as circumstances will carry him. Imputations not favorable to his integrity as a man rest upon him, but I do not vouch for their authenticity."[10]

Hamilton's hatred of Burr was a strange thing. In their personal relations they continued outwardly friendly. Although Burr, a supremely intelligent man, undoubtedly recognized that in politics Hamilton regarded him as an enemy, he seems to have gauged neither the depth of Hamilton's feeling nor the extremes to which Hamilton would resort to express it. Indeed it was probably Hamilton's good fortune that his opinions did not become public at this point, for this was an age in which the code duello still governed questions of honor and duels were fought over smaller provocations than his epistolatory statements about Burr.

The code duello was deeply rooted in the whole concept of the gentleman. The duel may have originated when individuals battled for their respective peoples — the contest between David and Goliath is often considered such an instance. In the Middle Ages, knights jousted at tournaments and principals fought to determine their culpability for a crime, the victor establishing his innocence by his superior skill. Subsequently, when courts and laws were more available but somehow seemed inadequate as a recourse for vindicating one's honor, the duel developed as a means of settling personal questions between gentlemen. The Italians perfected the duel in all its elaborate arrangements in the sixteenth century, and the practice flourished throughout Europe for the next two hundred years. The Church strongly opposed it, while governments often struck sharply at duelists for taking the law into their own hands. Notwithstanding the strictures of Church and state and the loss of many thousands of lives, the duel persisted, and men prided themselves enormously on possessing a supple wrist and a dextrous sword arm, or on a keen eye and a steady hand with a pistol. The "gentleman" — as that last vestige of the knightly ideal was understood — was brought up to regard dueling as part of the code by which he lived. And both Burr and Hamilton regarded themselves as gentlemen.

But why did Hamilton feel as he did? For, so far as one can see, such intensity of emotion was largely on Hamilton's side, although this is another uncertainty since Burr, urbane and self-contained, rarely indulged in an extravagant oral or written display of his sentiments. If he did so in this case, the documents have not survived. In reality the two rivals had numerous similarities. Both were slight of build and of only medium stature, Hamilton five feet seven inches, Burr an inch shorter. Both were delicate of feature, handsome, smartly dressed, often gay, and gracious in manner — Burr unfailingly so. The loose gossip of the period, with whatever justification or lack of it, named both as notable ladies' men.

But they were men's men too. They hunted and rode, challenged offenders to duels long before they confronted each other at Weehawken, and by a curious alchemy of intellectual vigor and attractiveness of personality won friends who remained loyal through the trying events of their lives. Both had seen hard and honorable service in the Revolution, and each retained a lively interest in military affairs. Both were brilliant lawyers, and both had soaring political ambitions, although Hamilton's were first to mature and remained easier to identify. Both, furthermore, had political astuteness in the manipulation of men and parties. Perhaps it was in part these very similarities that proved fatal to any possibility of real friendship; they simply got in each other's way.

Their differences, however, were fully as striking. Hamilton had risen from the ignominy of bastardy to fame and position by acuteness of intellect, a fortunate marriage, and a solid commitment to a conception of government and society that found favor with the most influential, if not the most numerous, part of the population. He had been an indefatigable and constructive force in the formation of national policy. Burr, coming from an eminently respectable background, if one tainted by mental illness on his mother's side, had taken a much more leisurely view toward life; he had, in fact, made no political contribution that even approached Hamilton's. Moreover, the peculiar circumstances of his bringing up and the natural inclination of his mind made him something of a lone wolf; though socially attractive and popular, he always preserved an inward aloofness and independence. Both were great lawyers; Hamilton never failed to emphasize the legal principles involved in the cases he presented, while Burr pounced on the weaknesses in his opponents' evidence or reasoning. In politics Hamilton sought to inspire men primarily by the force of his ideas and the logic of his argument; Burr bored immediately into the area of their self-interest. The irony in their political views is worth reiteration: Hamilton, who had been a nobody, insisted personally and through his party on the right of the rich and well-born to govern; Burr, born a colonial aristocrat, believed in or at least became an important member of a party that believed in the equality of man.

It has been suggested that Hamilton's hatred of Burr was pathological. Perhaps it was. Certainly it persisted for many years on the deep level below the amenities of social intercourse. A psychiatrist could probably make out a good case of insecurity on the part of both men, but one more apparent, if not more real, for Hamilton. Three times Burr had threatened Hamilton's political control — by his displacement of Schuyler in the Senate, his part in Jay's defeat as governor, and now his movement to gain the vice-presidency of the United States. That Burr received little support from the Republicans, who cast for Clinton, the ultimate loser to Adams, made little difference in Hamilton's feeling. Burr, in his opinion, remained a menace to Hamilton's own Federalist Party, to the nation's policies of which he, Hamilton, had been one of the principal architects, and to the very structure of the national government. At the same time, however genuine Hamilton's alarm, the lengths to which he went to thwart Burr hardly did justice to the quality of his mind or character. His strident, utterly sweeping denunciations, suggesting in their tone an underlying personal antipathy, tend to stir one's sympathy for Burr, who, preserving an enigmatic silence ("a grave sort of animal," Burr described himself[11]), really neither needs sympathy nor, perhaps, deserves it.

But these two brilliant men were not finished with frustrating each other. When the question of a successor to Gouverneur Morris as minister to France arose, the Republicans in Congress wanted Burr; and a small committee which included Madison and Monroe went to Washington with the recommendation. Washington said that he had never recommended or appointed to a high office a man in whose integrity he had no confidence; hence he could not accept Burr. Twice more the committee visited him, and the third time he refused to see them. In Washington's attitude, whether justifiably or not, men saw the hand of Hamilton — who, unlike Burr, had long ago made his peace with "The Great man," as he had once sneeringly alluded to the commander in chief.[12]

A change of status presently occurred for both men. Hamilton resigned from the Cabinet in late 1795, and was thereafter able to attend more closely to political management of Federalist fortunes. In the Presidential election of 1796 the Republicans supported a Jefferson-Burr team, but Jefferson lost to John Adams by three electoral votes, while Burr, with thirty votes, was thirty-eight short of Jefferson. Actually Jefferson, who in his way was as distrustful of Burr as was Hamilton, dominated Virginia so completely that only one vote from that state was cast for Burr, an "event," Hamilton said, that "will not a little mortify Burr."[13] The Jeffersonians, a prominent Federalist wrote before the election, "doubtless respect Burr's talents, but they dread his independence of *them*."[14] Beset within his own party, Burr thus lost the vice-presidency, and in three months — thanks to Hamilton's management from the outside — found himself ejected from the Senate by a powerful combination in the New York Legislature. Back to the Senate went General Schuyler, Hamilton's father-in-law, and back to New York as a private citizen went Burr.

In the spring of 1797, Burr was elected by New York City to the Assembly, and while waiting for the opening, he found himself involved in a most peculiar relationship with Hamilton. The latter had discharged his duties as Secretary of the Treasury with a probity that even Burr did not seriously question. Now suddenly a scurrilous Republican journalist published documents purporting to show Hamilton guilty of theft and fraud. Actually the case against him was spurious. One of its aspects, however, was a sensational revelation of his intimacy with a Mrs. James Reynolds. Back in 1791–1792, Hamilton had indeed become involved in an affair with the flashy Maria Reynolds, whose husband, conniving with her, worked Hamilton for blackmail. When Hamilton at last realized that he was being victimized, he revealed the whole story to three members of Congress, one of whom was James Monroe. Although he had in fact paid out a good deal of money, he satisfied the congressmen that it was not

Aaron Burr, 1802, by John Vanderlyn.
Courtesy of The New-York Historical Society, New York City.

drawn from public funds. The three men pledged their secrecy, and Hamilton gave them the papers. Now in 1797 the secret was a secret no longer, and Hamilton was understandably horrified.

He reacted promptly and courageously. He published a pamphlet explaining the situation and concealing few details. At the same time he was furious at the breach of confidence and held Monroe responsible. Although Monroe had indeed let the documents pass out of his keeping, he denied any culpability for their publication. In July, 1797, the two men had an argument, and Hamilton wrote Monroe a letter which the Virginian construed as a challenge to a duel. Monroe replied that if Hamilton meant to challenge, "I have then to request that you will say so, and in which case, have to inform you that my friend, Col. Burr, who will present you this . . . is authorized to give my answer to it, and to make such other arrangements as may be suitable in such an event."[15]

To Burr the incident must have seemed amusing and ironical. But he read the correspondence Monroe sent him, agreed to act as Monroe's second, and called on Hamilton. The latter was astonished; he had thought that Monroe was issuing a challenge! Burr then wrote out a statement of reconciliation which was accepted by both men.

That same year the breakdown of good relations between the United States and the French Republic brought national attention to the military establishment. President Adams called Washington away from Mount Vernon and appointed him commander of the army. Hamilton, at Washington's request, was made second in command. Scenting battle smoke, Burr eagerly offered his services. Adams proposed to Washington, and through him to the army triumvirate of Hamilton, Timothy Pickering, and Charles Pinckney, that Burr be nominated for brigadier general. According to Adams, Washington refused on the grounds that although Burr was "a brave and *able* officer," he had "equal talents at intrigue." Adams was astounded. He said of Washington, "He had compelled me to promote, over the heads of Lincoln, Gates, Clinton, Knox, and others, and even over Pinckney, one of his own triumvirate, the most restless, impatient, artful, indefatigable and unprincipled intriguer in the United States, if not in the world, to be second in command under himself, and now dreaded an intriguer in a poor brigadier! He did, however, propose it to the triumvirate, at least to Hamilton. But I was not permitted to nominate Burr."[16] Wherever Burr turned, he encountered a roadblock.

Burr kept Hamilton uneasy. In collaboration with the keeper of an upholstery shop, William Mooney, a Revolutionary veteran, he created a vital political force out of the social society which Mooney had founded in 1789, the Society of St. Tammany. Although Burr did not formally join Tammany nor ever enter the smoky, beery Wigwam, he became its real chief, and Mooney and the other braves took their orders from him or his lieutenants who joined the Society — men like Matthew Davis, John and William P. Van Ness, John and Robert Swartwout, and others. With the Tammany braves on the political warpath, meetings were regularly held in ward or local district, funds were collected by door-to-door canvass, and voters were induced by various means to do their duty. Soon Burr, emerging as one of the country's first city bosses, had a powerful political machine, which had no difficulty returning him and many Republicans to the Assembly in 1798. Federalist fears began to rise; Hamilton, it seemed to many in his party, was losing his hold to a new power.

Meanwhile Burr as an assemblyman was constructing a curious but interesting record that afforded

Hamilton no joy. He proposed a reform that would give the selection of Presidential electors to the voters rather than the Legislature. He demanded the abolition of slavery in New York. He proposed a freer bankruptcy law. He criticized the Alien and Sedition Acts. He supported the theory of states rights as embodied in the controversial Kentucky and Virginia Resolutions. He puzzled Federalists, who had forgotten his interest in military matters, by agreeably working with them in behalf of stronger fortifications for New York harbor. He also succeeded in getting through a law making it possible for aliens to hold land indefinitely. This greatly assisted the Dutch-controlled Holland Land Company, whose agent, Theophile Cazenove, would have been forced to lend Schuyler's Canal Company an exorbitant sum in return for a twenty-year restrictive law. Receiving no encouragement from Hamilton, Schuyler's partner, Cazenove went to Burr, who, employing all manner of inducements including bribery, secured a more liberal regulation from the Legislature. When John Barker Church, a brother-in-law to Hamilton, dropped some derogatory words about Burr's reward in this transaction, which was considerable though Burr denied it, Burr challenged him. Both principals escaped harm, but Church's bullet ripped through Burr's coat.

Another factor exacerbating relations between Hamilton and Burr pertained to banking. The two great banks in the State of New York, both under Federalist control, were the Bank of New York and a branch of the Bank of the United States. Hamilton had been especially instrumental in setting up the Bank of New York, of which he was a director. Now, after a number of years of monopoly, these banks were faced with a competitor established in the main by Burr. The Legislature had voted a charter to the Manhattan Company, which had been organized by Burr for the purpose of bringing "pure and wholesome water" to New York City. One paragraph in the charter, however, had a "sleeper" clause — namely, that surplus capital could be spent in any way not inconsistent with either the laws or the Constitution. Although the Manhattan Company, with a sturdy stock subscription, went to work in a limited way on the first necessary steps to provide the city with water, Burr quickly took advantage of the "sleeper" to create what was to become the great Bank of the Manhattan Company. Truly, as Chief Justice Morgan Lewis had pointed out to Governor Jay when the charter came up for his signature, the paragraph in question contained more than "pure and wholesome water"! At once Hamilton and the Federalists went into action, playing especially on the sensibilities of Republicans who were all too aware of Jefferson's opposition to banks. Hence in the elections of 1799 Burr and the city Republicans were ousted from the Assembly. But Burr's bank remained to trouble the Hamiltonians.

The local and national elections of 1800 again brought to a sharp focus the political rivalry of Hamilton and Burr. Since the legislatures chose the Presidential electors, it was essential that they be of the proper political complexion. The New England states were largely Federalist; the Southern states largely Republican; the Middle Atlantic states debatable, with New York holding the position of greatest strategic importance. On the face of it, New York looked Federalist in view of the striking Federalist victories in 1799. The Republicans, however, with Burr in the role of the astute and energetic political manager, put up a slate of their most able and well-known men, including old Governor Clinton and General Gates.

Although the Republican cause at first seemed hopeless, Hamilton inadvertently helped it. He distrusted President Adams almost as completely as he distrusted Jefferson or Burr, and he resolved to replace him with his friend Charles Cotesworth Pinckney. Since this replacement movement depended on the election of men whom he could control, he came up with an undistinguished list of candidates who roused little enthusiasm among the voters. Burr, on the other hand, was much more successful. Since the franchise was based on property, Republicans who had insufficient property or none at all were directed to buy blocks of property together so that as joint tenants they could qualify under the voting laws. Funds were collected on a methodical basis, orators harangued the people, and the Tammany war drums continued to roll. The result of this organized enthusiasm and a notable panel of candidates was a decisive Republican victory in both city and state, and Burr was its principal architect. Burr himself went to the Legislature from Orange County.

Faced with defeat, Hamilton tried to nullify the Republican victory by requesting Governor Jay to call a special session of the Federalist Legislature, which still had time in office, and to instruct the Legislature to authorize the election of the Presidential electors by popular vote rather than by the Legislature itself. This desperate suggestion was too much for Jay to swallow. Months earlier, the Republicans had advocated this very modification, but the Federalists, at Hamilton's direction, had defeated the proposal. Hamilton thus had no recourse now but to accept the Republican success in New York and to work for a Federalist victory in the Presidential election.

Unfortunately for his party, Hamilton drove a wedge into the ranks of the Federalists by his continued attacks on Adams. He wrote a pamphlet for the leaders of his party which was nothing short of a diatribe against Adams as a man unfit for his office. He kept the printing of the pamphlet a secret, but Burr, who had an efficient intelligence system, secured a fresh copy before it was distributed and sent it to the Republican newspapers. It would have been hard to tell whether the Republican reading public was more amused than the Federalists were angered. Hamilton was doing more to hurt the latter than either Jefferson or Burr.

Meanwhile, with the Republicans deciding on a ticket of Jefferson for President and Burr for vice-president, Hamilton struck back vigorously. To influential friends throughout the country he pointed out the dangers in Burr's ascendancy, using language that would again have been a dueling matter had it come to Burr's attention. He wrote James A. Bayard of Delaware that if Burr should become President he would "certainly attempt to reform the government *a la Bonaparte*. He is as unprincipled and dangerous a man as any country can boast — as true a Catiline as ever met in midnight conclave."[17] To John Rutledge of South Carolina he said that the idea of electing Burr, "one of the most unprincipled men in the United States," was "impolitic and impure."[18]

He did not stop here. With South Carolina throwing its electoral votes entirely to Jefferson and Burr, it was clear that the powerful Federalist hold on the Presidential office was at last broken, for Jefferson and Burr were given seventy-three electoral votes each, Adams sixty-five, Pinckney sixty-four, and Jay one. The tie for first place meant that the new President would be determined by the existing House of Representatives, which was Federalist and whose members initially, as individuals, showed a preference for Burr over Jefferson. This situation afforded Hamilton a magnificent opportunity to deliver the *coup de grace* to the man he was coming to hate, at least as a politician, more than anyone alive and whose motives —

there is no doubt of Hamilton's sincerity — he deeply distrusted. Accordingly he picked up his pen again.

He expressed himself as bluntly as ever in letters to Federalists, entreating them to use their influence to block Burr. He told Oliver Wolcott that no circumstance in political affairs ever gave him "so much pain" as the idea that Federalists might elect Burr President. Not only was Burr "one of the worst men in the community," but "Adieu to the Federal Troy, if they once introduce this Grecian horse into their citadel."[19] To Gouverneur Morris he faced squarely the question of choosing between his two political enemies, Jefferson and Burr. He admitted that if there was a man in the world he ought to hate, "it is Jefferson. With Burr I have always been personally well. But the public good must be paramount to every private consideration." Burr, "bankrupt beyond redemption," listened only to his ambition; he was a man who would use "the worst part of the community" to crush "the better part." Burr was "sanguine enough to hope every thing, daring enough to attempt every thing, wicked enough to scruple nothing."[20] To James Bayard again, Hamilton insisted that Burr "has no principle, public nor private. . . . For Heaven's sake, my dear sir, exert yourself to the utmost to save our country from so great a calamity."[21] When Theodore Sedgwick spoke out for Burr, Hamilton became distraught: "I beg of you, as you love your country, your friends, and yourself, to reconsider dispassionately the opinion you have expressed in favor of Burr. I never was so much mistaken as I shall be if our friends, in the event of their success, do not rue the preference they will give to that *Catiline*."[22]

Hamilton, however, learned to his dismay that all his frantic efforts were in vain, and he sadly acknowledged that his influence with the Federalists was gone. Indeed the Federalists were put out with him for splitting the party. They also feared Burr far less than their old enemy, Jefferson. They even thought they could bring Burr to their side, and they fought as hard for him in the House as the Republicans had earlier at the polls. Thirty-six ballots were taken before the nation acquired a new President who was not Burr, among other reasons because Burr declined to make concessions to the Federalists, who regretfully concluded that Jefferson would be the less dangerous man. Bayard and Congressman William Cooper — both Federalists — admitted that Burr could have had the election had he cooperated; in fact, on the first ballot, though Jefferson had eight states to Burr's six, Burr had fifty-five individual votes to Jefferson's fifty-one. But Burr, standing on a no-commitment policy, preferred to play the lone wolf to the last. Hence, with the Republicans voting heavily for Jefferson and enough Federalists abstaining, Jefferson was finally elected President and Burr vice-president. In consequence of the impasse over the election, the Twelfth Amendment to the Constitution was adopted in 1804, preventing such a situation in the future.

Both Hamilton and Burr presently suffered personal griefs, Hamilton's being especially poignant. His oldest son, Philip, had a political quarrel with George Eacker, a young Republican lawyer, in November, 1801, and challenged him to a duel. At a first meeting the shots of both men went wild, but at a second meeting Eacker mortally wounded young Hamilton. Not only did Hamilton thus lose his son, who was his brightest hope, but the event drove his oldest daughter insane.

Burr's grief was hardly of the same nature or depth, although it was acute. The dearest person in his life after the death of his wife was their daughter Theodosia. Clever and graceful, exhibiting a charm and poise that made her father proud, she acted as his hostess at his Manhattan estate, Richmond Hill. She was equally gracious to great and humble but was particularly interested in the meetings of Burr's political henchmen, whom, with memories of her readings in Ceasar's account of the Gallic wars, she called "the Tenth Legion." During the balloting in the House of Representatives she married rich young Joseph Alston of South Carolina, who summered in the Hudson River country. He was by no means her match in intellect or personality, and the suspicion still lingers that Burr persuaded Alston to propose and the seventeen-year-old Theodosia to accept in order to establish an affluent and politically influential connection that might be helpful to him. If Theodosia ever suspected her father, she remained nevertheless loyal and devoted. "I had rather not live," she wrote Burr later on, "than not be the daughter of such a man."[23] Yet not even his enemies doubted the sincerity of the wrench he felt at her departure for the South. In all her absence he never permitted anyone to occupy her chair at the dining table and always had a place-setting laid for her.

By no means did Hamilton and Burr permit their private sorrow to inhibit their continued active interest in politics. Burr, after all, was vice-president of the United States and, as such, president of the Senate. Men were warm in their praise of him as a presiding officer. This was a needed balm, for he was finding Jefferson almost as difficult as Hamilton. With many of the Federalists drawn to Burr and with Burr acting at times as if he wished to court such attention, Jefferson did not trust the New Yorker. Burr, he once said, was like "a crooked gun or other perverted machine, whose aim or shot you could never be sure of."[24] Jefferson rarely consulted him and did not invite him to

Cabinet meetings. Burr therefore soon felt useless in the government. Actually he was experiencing only to an accentuated degree the frustration that has torn at the self-respect of so many men who have held his unenviable office — "the most insignificant," John Adams had said disgustedly, "that ever the mind of man contrived or his imagination conceived."[25] For one of Burr's consummate ability, a man moreover who had been largely responsible for the Republican victory, the situation was intolerable. Small wonder that he turned his attention increasingly to New York. There at least he counted for something.

In New York, however, he found Hamilton ready as ever to oppose his designs, particularly through a newspaper Hamilton had helped set up — the *Evening Post,* edited by William Coleman, a former law partner of Burr himself. He also discovered a new satellite in the heavens. This was DeWitt Clinton, nephew of the old governor, who was eager to perpetuate the Republican dynasty in his own name. Thanks in part to him, but with the assistance of all Republican factions that hated the Tammany boss, a scathing newspaper war against Burr broke out. It was spearheaded by the *American Citizen,* whose radical editor James Cheetham became a Clinton tool. Furthermore, through DeWitt Clinton, who had resigned from the Senate and had taken over the mayoralty of New York City, Jefferson learned of the plans of the Clintons and Livingstons to break the power of the Burr faction, which was pushing its leader for governor of New York in the election to be held in late April, 1804. Jefferson, while professing neutrality, was not sorry to see Burr's power diminished, and he notified the latter's New York Republican enemies of what he knew of the Colonel's plans.

For Hamilton, who was engaged in a Homeric but vain defense of a Federalist editor who had reprinted a libel on Jefferson, the spectacle of a divided Republicanism was by no means reassuring. He felt that Burr, who at first preserved a contemptuous silence amid the attacks against him, was still very strong despite Jefferson, the Clintons, and the Livingstons. And Hamilton was right. In February, 1804, enthusiasm ran high for Burr both in the city and upstate, and a stinging pamphlet against his enemies by William Van Ness was being gleefully discussed. Opposed to Burr was the Clinton-Livingston machine, the regular organization, but its managers were troubled. Their nominee, Chancellor Lansing, at first accepted, then resigned when he realized that his nomination could not reconcile the Republican factions. The bosses now turned to a Livingston man, Morgan Lewis, a Revolutionary War veteran and the Chief Justice. Still, Lewis faced the prospect that a good many Republicans, and Federalists as well, would vote for Burr.

The Federalists, especially the New Englanders, were indeed looking at Burr with friendly eyes. Hamilton appeared to have failed them completely as their leader. He even viewed the Jeffersonian purchase of Louisiana with equanimity, compared with their own outlook. Theirs was a sectional prejudice based on an aversion both to the dominance of Virginia and, given the acquisition of Louisiana, to the inevitability of their own section's shrinking in political and economic importance. In their concern, a number of prominent New England Federalists considered secession. Their conviction that the success of the movement depended upon the support of New York led them to consult Burr with the hope of bringing him to their persuasion. To their chagrin, they could not pin him down. Senator William Plumer of New Hampshire observed that nothing Burr said could be construed as necessarily approving secession. Congressman Roger Griswold of Connecticut, meeting with

Burr, learned only that the Vice-President was bitterly resentful of Virginian domination and that "he must go on democratically to obtain the government; that, if he succeeded, he should administer it in a manner that would be satisfactory to the Federalists."[26] This was scant encouragement to Griswold and Plumer, and to fellow conspirators such as Senator Timothy Pickering of Massachusetts and Senators James Hillhouse and Uriah Tracy of Connecticut. Notwithstanding their disappointment, they endeavored in every way to persuade their fellow Federalists in New York to vote for Burr, and drank many a toast to "Aaron's rod — may it blossom in New York!"

With the apple of discord thus polished brightly in both parties, Hamilton, initially reluctant to enter the campaign, now sought with every resource at his command to accomplish the defeat of Aaron Burr. Although somewhat handicapped in the use of the press by the strange abstention of the *Post*'s editor, Coleman, from partisanship in his behalf, he wrote numerous letters and talked with many people. To a secret meeting of Federalists in Albany, before Lansing's withdrawal, he pointed out that the effect of Burr's election "will be to reunite under a more adroit, able, and daring chief, the now scattered fragments of the Democratic party [the name the Republicans were eventually to adopt], and to reinforce it by a strong detachment from the Federalists." He felt that it would probably suit Burr to see a dismemberment of the Union, particularly if he could become chief of the northern part. This "man of irregular and unsatiable ambition" must be stopped.[27]

To the surprise of the Federalists who attended the conclave, Burr's newspaper, the *Morning Chronicle,* through which Burr was now belatedly attempting to strike back at his enemies, published a full account of their proceedings. Two Burr spies had hidden under a bed in a room adjoining the banquet hall. Burr thus learned that although Hamilton had insisted he would take no active part in the campaign, he was certainly in it in secret. And indeed he continued to write to individuals and to speak at private dinners.

One such talk he gave at a dinner as the guest of Judge John Tayler in Albany. Some of his remarks on that occasion, embodied in a letter written by Tayler's son-in-law Dr. Charles D. Cooper to General Schuyler, found their way into print in the *Albany Register* — and by this means came eventually to Burr's attention.

Although many Federalists made up their minds to vote for Burr, one Federalist congressman considering Hamilton's antagonism to Burr as springing from personal resentment, the anti-Burrites among the Federalists and the pro-Lewis Republicans crushed Burr in a landslide, 30,829 votes to 22,139. Yet Burr could write to Theodosia, "The election is lost by a great majority: *tant mieux.*"[28]

But the result rankled, regardless of his attempts to be philosophical. Two men he believed responsible for his defeat — DeWitt Clinton and Alexander Hamilton, the latter particularly. That belief, and Cooper's letter to General Schuyler, led directly to the Hudson's shore in Weehawken on the bright morning of July 11, 1804.

Notes

1. Hamilton was born on St. Kitts, the illegitimate son of James Hamilton and Rachel Lavien, née Fawcett. Most scholars now assign 1755 rather than 1757 as the year of his birth, but Hamilton alluded to himself as nineteen years old when he received his commission as captain in the American army. The precise year will probably remain a matter of debate.

Biographies and special studies of Hamilton are legion and of varying quality. Perhaps the most scholarly and most thorough is Broadus Mitchell, *Alexander Ham-*

ilton ([2] vols., New York, 1957–). Two recent biographies are: Nathan Schachner, *Alexander Hamilton* (New York, 1946; special edition, 1957) and John C. Miller, *Alexander Hamilton: Portrait in Paradox* (New York, 1959).

2. Burr was born in 1756, son of the Reverend Aaron Burr, who became president of Princeton, and Esther Edwards, daughter of the theologian of the Great Awakening, Jonathan Edwards. By the time Burr was little more than two years old, both his parents were dead of smallpox; his grandfather Edwards, called to succeed his son-in-law as the Princeton president, died of an inoculation for smallpox; while his grandmother, Sarah Edwards, perished of dysentery. Temporarily cared for by the Shippen family of Philadelphia, Burr and his sister Sally soon became wards of their uncle Timothy Edwards, their mother's oldest brother, who made his home for a time in Elizabethtown, New Jersey. Tapping Reeve, who tutored Burr and whom Sally married, became the first chief justice of the Supreme Court of Connecticut.

Biographies of Burr, though numerous, usually suffer from attempts that are carried to extremes to explain and defend him. The most convincing biography, one definitely pro-Burr but restrained and judicious, is Nathan Schachner, *Aaron Burr* (New York, 1937). Also of great value is the work of Samuel H. Wandell and Meade Minnegerode, *Aaron Burr* (2 vols., New York, 1925). A useful biography, fundamentally serious despite a certain facetiousness of tone, and one in which the author eschews the role of devil's advocate, is Holmes Alexander, *Aaron Burr, the Proud Pretender* (New York, 1937).

3. For the incident, see Matthew L. Davis, *Memoirs of Aaron Burr with Miscellaneous Selections from His Correspondence* (2 vols., New York, 1837), I, 100–105; see also "Mulligan's Narrative," in Hamilton Papers, Library of Congress.

4. Burr to Washington, July 21, 1777. Davis, *op. cit.*, I, 111.

5. Hamilton to Philip Schuyler, February 18, 1781. Morristown National Historical Park, Morristown, New Jersey. (References to manuscripts in these notes are refer-

ences to photostats of the originals, located in the Papers of Alexander Hamilton, Columbia University, New York City.)

6. For James Kent's descriptions of Hamilton and Burr, see his addresses to the Law Association of the City of New York for 1832 and 1836, excerpted in Charles Warren, *History of the American Bar* (Boston, 1911), 295–300.

7. J[ames]. Parton, *The Life and Times of Aaron Burr* (New York, 1858), 152–153.

8. Hamilton to an unknown correspondent, September 21, 1792. Hamilton Papers, Library of Congress.

9. Hamilton to an unknown correspondent, September 26, 1792. Hamilton Papers, Library of Congress.

10. Hamilton to Charles Cotesworth Pinckney, October 10, 1792 (Charleston Library Society, Charleston, South Carolina); and Hamilton to John Steele, October 15, 1792 (University of North Carolina, Chapel Hill, North Carolina).

11. *The Private Journal of Aaron Burr,* edited by Matthew L. Davis (2 vols., New York, 1838), II, 425.

12. Hamilton to James McHenry, February 18, 1781. James McHenry Papers, Library of Congress.

13. Hamilton to Rufus King, December 16, 1796. New-York Historical Society.

14. Theodore Sedgwick to Jonathan Dayton, November 19, 1796. Quoted in Schachner, *Alexander Hamilton* (New York, 1957), 357.

15. James Monroe to Hamilton, August 6, 1797. Morristown National Historical Park, Morristown, New Jersey.

16. *The Works of John Adams,* edited by Charles Francis Adams (12 vols. Boston, 1874–1877), IX, 294.

17. Hamilton to James Bayard, August 6, 1800. Bayard Letterbook, New York Public Library.

18. Hamilton to John Rutledge, January 4, 1801. Hamilton Papers, Library of Congress.

19. Hamilton to Oliver Wolcott [December, 1800]. Connecticut Historical Society.

20. Hamilton to Gouverneur Morris, December 26 and 24, 1800. Hamilton Papers, Library of Congress.

21. Hamilton to James A. Bayard, December 27, 1800. Bayard Letterbook, New York Public Library.

22. Hamilton to Theodore Sedgwick, January 21, 1801. Hamilton Papers, Library of Congress.

23. Davis, *op. cit.,* I, 285.

24. Thomas Jefferson, *The Complete Anas,* edited by F. B. Sawvel (New York, 1903), 227.

25. Louis Clinton Hatch, *A History of the Vice-Presidency of the United States,* revised and edited by Earl L. Shoup (New York, 1934), 53.

26. Quoted in Schachner, *Aaron Burr,* 244–245.

27. Speech by Alexander Hamilton at a Meeting of Federalists in Albany, February 10, 1804. Hamilton Papers, Library of Congress.

28. Burr to Theodosia Burr Alston, May 1, 1804. Quoted in Davis, *Memoirs of Aaron Burr,* II, 285.

Interview in Weehawken

THE DOCUMENTS

William P. Van Ness's Account of the Events of June 18, 1804[1]

On the afternoon of the 17th June last I received a Note[2] from Col: Burr requesting me to call on him the following morning which I did. Upon my arrival he observed that it had of late been frequently stated to him that Genl Hamilton had at different times and upon various occasions used language and expressed opinions highly injurious to his reputation, that he had for some time felt the necessity of calling on Genl Hamilton for some explanation of his conduct, but that the statements which had been made to him, did not appear sufficiently au-

1. "Van Ness's Narrative," AD, New York State Historical Association, Cooperstown, N.Y.

Aaron Burr selected William P. Van Ness to carry on the negotiations with Alexander Hamilton and later to serve as Burr's second in the duel with Hamilton. Van Ness, a protégé and political associate of Burr, had begun the practice of law in New York City in 1800.

Van Ness wrote a narrative of the negotiations between Burr and Hamilton which was printed with minor changes in wording in the New York *Morning Chronicle,* July 17, 1804. The narrative as printed in the *Morning Chronicle* was preceded by the following statement:

> The gentleman who accompanied Col. Burr to the field in the late unfortunate contest, comes forward reluctantly with a statement on the subject, at a moment when any publication of the kind may expose his principal to judicial embarrassment, perhaps to very serious hazard.
>
> In the following narrative, he disclaims the most distant idea of injuring the memory of the deceased, for whom, while living, he entertained sentiments of high respect, and for whose melancholy exit he, as also

thentic to justify the measure. That a Newspaper[3] had however very recently been put into his hands in which he perceived a letter signed Ch: D. Cooper[4] containing information, which he thought demanded immediate investigation. Urged by these circumstances and justified by the opinion of his friends, he said, that he had determined to write Genl Hamilton a Note upon the subject which he requested me to deliver. I assented to his request, and on my return to the City which was at 11 O clock the same morning, I delivered to Genl Hamilton the Note[5] which I received from Col: Burr for that purpose & of which the following is a Copy.

---

his principal, feels particular regret. The task devolved on him by the duties of his situation shall be discharged with fidelity, but with every delicacy the circumstances of the case can claim.

In the New York State Historical Association there is a manuscript of the draft of this narrative as well as the manuscript of the narrative itself. In the footnotes in this volume, these two manuscripts have been entitled "Van Ness's Narrative" and "Draft of Van Ness's Narrative."

2. Note not found.

3. *The Albany Register,* April 24, 1804.

4. See Dr. Charles Cooper to Philip Schuyler, April 23, 1804, enclosure in Burr to Hamilton, June 18, 1804; see also Burr to Hamilton, June 18, 1804, note 1.

5. See Burr to Hamilton, June 18, 1804.

Aaron Burr to Alexander Hamilton[1]

N York 18 June 1804

Sir

I send for your perusal a letter[2] signed Ch. D. Cooper which, though apparently published some time ago, has but very recently come to my knowledge. Mr Van Ness who does me the favor to deliver this, will point out to you that clause of the letter to which I particularly request your attention.[3]

You must perceive, Sir, the Necessity of a prompt and unqualified acknowledgment or denial of the use of any expressions which could warrant the assertions of Dr. Cooper

I have the honor to be
Your Obdt s^t
A. Burr

Genl. Hamilton

1. ALS, New-York Historical Society; also ADf or copy in handwriting of Van Ness in New York State Historical Association, Cooperstown, N.Y.

This letter was written as a result of some derogatory remarks made by Hamilton about Burr at a dinner in the home of Judge John Tayler, of Albany. Among the guests at the dinner was Dr. Charles D. Cooper, Tayler's son-in-law, who subsequently wrote two letters describing Hamilton's conversation. The first of these letters, dated April 12, 1804, was addressed to Andrew Brown in Berne, a small town nineteen miles west of Albany. Brown was a prominent merchant in Albany. The second letter, dated April 23, 1804, was addressed to Philip Schuyler, Hamilton's father-in-law. Both letters were published in *The Albany Register*. It was the second of these two letters that Burr enclosed to Hamilton.

[*Enclosure*]

Dr. Charles Cooper to Philip Schuyler[4]

[Albany, April 23, 1804]

SIR,

THE malignant attack which my character has sustained in an anonymous hand-bill, to which your letter of the 21st inst.[5] directed to the chairman of the Federal electioneering committee of this city is annexed; and in which you contradict certain facts contained in a letter, said to have been

2. See enclosure printed below.

3. The clause to which Burr referred reads, ". . . really sir, I could detail to you a still more despicable opinion which General HAMILTON has expressed of Mr. BURR." See enclosure.

4. *The Albany Register,* April 24, 1804.

5. Philip Schuyler to Samuel Stringer, April 21, 1804. This letter was printed in *The Albany Register,* April 24, 1804.

Stringer was chairman of the Federal Republican Committee. In his letter to Stringer, Schuyler wrote that he had seen Cooper's letter to Andrew Brown and that he denied the accuracy of its facts concerning the political views of Hamilton, Stephen Van Rensselaer, and James Kent. Both Van Rensselaer and Kent were leading New York Federalists. Van Rensselaer, the eighth patroon, was Hamilton's brother-in-law. Kent was a justice of the New York Supreme Court.

Schuyler's letter dealt with the thoroughly confused political situation in New York. In February, 1804, the Burr faction of the state Democratic party had nominated Burr for governor. The anti-Burr branch of the party nominated Chancellor John Lansing as its candidate. When Lansing withdrew from the race, the anti-Burrites

44

written by me to ANDREW BROWN,[6] Esq. of Bern, will be my apology for repelling the unfounded aspersions which have been thus dishonorably obtruded on the public. My letter to Mr. BROWN was committed to the care of JOHAN J. DEITZ, Esq. of Bern; but to this gentleman, I hope, cannot be imputed the embezzling and breaking open of a letter, a crime which in England has met with the most ignominious punishment.

Admitting the letter published to be a exact transcript of the one intended for Mr. BROWN, and which, it seems, instead of being delivered accord-

---

nominated Morgan Lewis, chief justice of the state supreme court. The Federalists did not nominate a candidate, and the party was divided over whether to support Burr or Lewis. The letters by Schuyler and Cooper were concerned with the problem of which Democratic candidate the state's leading Federalists would support.

6. Charles Cooper's letter to Andrew Brown reads as follows:

Albany, 12th April, 1804

Dear Sir,

You will receive some election papers, and some of them in the German language. I presume you will make use of them to the best advantage: have them dispersed and scattered as much as possible. The friends of Col. Burr are extremely active, and will require all our exertion to put them down. It is believed that most of the reflecting Federalists will vote for Lewis. Gen. Hamilton, the patroon's brother-in-law, it is said, has come out decidedly against Burr; indeed when he was here he spoke of him as a dangerous man, and who ought not to be trusted. Judge Kent also expressed the same sentiment. The patroon was quite indifferent about it when he went to New-York.

ing to promise, was EMBEZZLED AND BROKEN OPEN; I aver, that the assertions therein contained are substantially true, and that I can prove them by the most unquestionable testimony. I assert, that Gen. HAMILTON and Judge KENT have declared, in substance, that they looked upon Mr. BURR to be a dangerous man, and one who ought not to be trusted with the reins of government. If, Sir, you attended a meeting of federalists, at the city tavern, where Gen. HAMILTON made a speech on the pending election, I might appeal to you for the truth of so much of this assertion as relates to him. I have, however, other evidence to substantiate the fact. With respect to Judge KENT's declaration, I have only to refer to THEODORUS V. W. GRAHAM,[7] Esq. and Mr. JAMES KANE,[7] of this city, whose veracity, I trust, will not be impeached; but should the fact

---

It is thought when he sees Gen. Hamilton and his brother-in-law Mr. Church (who Burr some time ago fought a duel with, and of course, must bear Burr much hatred) I say many feel persuaded that Mr. Renselaer will be decidedly opposed to Mr. Burr. If you think any of us can aid you in the election in your town let us know and we will give you what assistance is in our power; can you send me word what you think will be the result of the election in your town?

Yours sincerely,
Chars. D. Cooper

A. Brown, Esq.

Perhaps it will be of use to shew the part of this letter that relates to the Patroon, Hamilton and Church, to some of the Patroon [s] tenants. I leave it to your discretion. In haste (reprinted from *The Albany Register* in the *New-York Evening Post,* July 23, 1804).

have escaped their recollection, I am not in want of other evidence, equally respectable, to support it. Mr. VAN RENSSELAER, a few days before he left town for New-York, in a conversation with me, declared in substance what I communicated in the letter to Mr. BROWN, as coming from him; and I am perfectly willing to repose myself on his well-known candour for the truth of this declaration.

I asserted, in the letter which has been so disgracefully EMBEZZLED, AND THE BREAKING OPEN of which must be ranked with the lowest species of villainy, that many of the reflecting federalists would support Judge LEWIS. Will this be considered a rash assertion, when it is known that two federal gentlemen, high in office in this city, have declared they would vote for him? Judge PENDLETON, of New-York, made the same declaration in this city, under the impression, however, that no federal candidate was to be offered. OLIVER PHELPS,[8] when in this city, on his way to Canandaigua, stated, that Gen. HAMILTON, and about one hundred federalists in New-York, would not vote for Mr. BURR.

It is true, that Judge TAYLER intimated to me, the conversation Mr. VAN RENSSELAER had with him, to which you allude, but it was subsequent to my having written and dispatched the letter for Mr. BROWN.

---

7. Theodorus V. W. Graham was an Albany lawyer and politician. James Kane was an Albany merchant.

8. Oliver Phelps, a large landowner in Ontario County, had been nominated for lieutenant governor on the Burr ticket.

I beg leave to remark, sir, that the anxiety you discovered, when his Honor the Chancellor was about to be nominated, induced me to believe, that you entertained a bad opinion of Mr. BURR, especially when taken in connection with General HAMILTON's harangue at the city tavern;[9] and although I have never suggested that you would act on the one side or the other in this election — yet, presuming on the correctness of your mind, and the reputation you sustain of an upright and exemplary character, I could not suppose you would support a man whom I had reason to believe, you held in the lowest estimation.

It is sufficient for me, on this occasion, to substantiate what I have asserted. I have made it an invariable rule of my life, to be circumspect in relating what I may have heard from others; and in this affair, I feel happy to think, that I have been unusually cautious — for really sir, I could detail to you a still more despicable opinion which General HAMILTON has expressed of Mr. BURR.

I cannot conclude, without paying some attention to your friend, Dr. STRINGER; I have to regret that this gentleman, so renowned for the Christian virtues, should have consented to dishonour your name, by connecting your letter with an anony-

9. At the time that the Federalists were divided over which Democratic candidate to support, Hamilton was in Albany arguing the Croswell libel case. During his stay in Albany, he attended a Federalist meeting at Lewis' Tavern in that city. Although this meeting was ostensibly called to support Burr, Hamilton used it as an occasion for an outspoken attack against Burr.

48

mous production, replete with the vilest falsehood and the foulest calumny.

> I am, Sir, with due respect,
> Your humble servant,
> CHARLES D. COOPER

April 23, 1804.

William P. Van Ness's Account of the Events of June 18–21, 1804[1]

Genl Hamilton read the Note of Mr Burr[2] and the printed letter of Mr Cooper to which it refers, and remarked that they required some consideration, and that in the course of the day he would send a answer to my office. At ½ past 1 O clock Genl Hamilton called at my house and said that a variety of engagements would demand his attention during the whole of that day and the next, but that on Wednesday the 20th Inst: he would furnish me

1. "Van Ness's Narrative," AD, New York State Historical Association, Cooperstown, N.Y.

In the draft of his "Narrative," Van Ness describes Hamilton's reaction to Burr's letter in the following words:

1804   June 18, Delivered a copy of the letter on the other side written to Genl Hamilton at 11 oclock A.M.

Genl Hamilton upon examining the letter alluded to by Col. Burr, & signed C. D. Cooper observed, that he did not think that the publication in question authorised Col. Burr to call upon him in the way he had, that its language and its references were so general and undefined that he did not perceive how he could with propriety return a specific answer to Col Burr's letter. That if Mr Burr would refer to any *particular expressions* he would recognize or disavow them. I remarked that I did not think Mr Burr was prepared to point out any specific & exceptionable language that had been used by him Mr Hamilton, but that the publication of Mr Cooper evidently alluded to expressions made by Mr Hamilton derogatory to the character and reputation of Mr Burr, and that the laws of honor would justify Mr Burr, in enquiring of any gentleman whether he had uttered expressions that imparted dis-

with such answer to Col: Burr's letter as he should deem most suitable and compatible with his feelings.

In the evening of Wednesday the 20th while I was from home, the following letter addressed to Col: Burr[3] was left at my house under cover to me. On the morning of Thursday the 21st I delivered to Col: Burr the above letter.[4]

---

honor. M[r] Hamilton said that he did not think my position correct, that he would examine the publication in question, and return me an answer in the course of the day.

P.M. At half past one oclock Genl Hamilton called at my house in person, and said that a variety of engagements would demand his attention through this day and tomorrow, but that on wednesday he would return such answer to M[r] Burr's letter as he should deem most suitable and compatible with his feelings. That he was sorry M[r] Burr had adopted the present course, that it was a subject that required some deliberation, and that he wished to proceed with justifiable caution and circumspection.

On Wednesday morning I saw Genl Hamilton in Court; He told me that I should be furnished with an answer to Col Burr's letter in the course of the afternoon. I assented very readily to the delay. I remained at home most of the afternoon, at 8 o clock I went out and during my absence the letter of which N[o]. 2 [Hamilton to Burr, June 20, 1804] is a copy was left at my house.

I delivered the same to Col Burr on the morning of thursday the 21. Instant.

2. Burr to Hamilton, June 18, 1804.
3. Hamilton to Burr, June 20, 1804.
4. *Ibid.*

Alexander Hamilton to Aaron Burr[1]

New York June 20, 1804

Sir

I have maturely reflected on the subject of your letter of the 18th instant; and the more I have reflected the more I have become convinced, that I could not, without manifest impropriety, make the avowal or disavowal which you seem to think necessary.

The clause pointed out by Mr Van Ness is in these terms, "I could detail to you a *still more despicable opinion,* which General Hamilton has expressed of Mr Burr." To endeavour to discover the meaning of this declaration, I was obliged to seek in the antecedent part of the letter for the opinion to which it referred, as having been already disclosed. I found it in these words "General Hamilton and Judge Kent have declared, *in substance,* that they looked upon M^r. Burr to be *a dangerous man,* and one *who ought not to be trusted with the reins of Government.*" The language of Doctor Cooper plainly implies, that he considered this opinion of you, which he attributes to me, as a *despicable* one; but he affirms that I have expressed some other *still more despicable;* without however mentioning to whom, when, or where. 'Tis evident, that the phrase "still more despicable" admits of infinite shades, from very light to very dark. How am I to judge of the degree intended? Or how

1. ALS, New York State Historical Association, Cooperstown, N.Y.; also ADf, New-York Historical Society. There is also a copy in the writing of Van Ness, New York State Historical Association.

shall I annex any precise idea to language so indefinite?

Between Gentlemen, *despicable* and *more despicable* are not worth the pains of a distinction. When therefore you do not interrogate me, as to the opinion which is specifically ascribed to me, I must conclude, that you view it as within the limits, to which the animadversions of political opponents, upon each other, may justifiably extend; and consequently as not warranting the idea of it, which Doctor Cooper appears to entertain. If so, what precise inference could you draw as a guide for your future conduct, were I to acknowlege, that I had expressed an opinion of you, *still more despicable,* than the one which is particularised? How could you be sure, that even this opinion had exceeded the bounds which you would yourself deem admissible between political opponents?

But I forbear further comment on the embarrassment to which the requisition you have made naturally leads. The occasion forbids a more ample illustration, though nothing would be more easy than to pursue it.

Repeating, that I cannot reconcile it with propriety to make the acknowlegement, or denial, you desire, I will add, that I deem it inadmissible, on principle, to consent to be interrogated as to the justness of the *inferences,* which may be drawn by *others,* from whatever I may have said of a political opponent in the course of a fifteen years competition. If there were no other objection to it, this is sufficient, that it would tend to expose my sincerity and delicacy to injurious imputations from every person, who may at any time have conceived the import of my expressions differently from what I may then have intended, or may afterwards recollect.

I stand ready to avow or disavow promptly and explicitly any precise or definite opinion, which I may be charged with having declared of any Gentleman. More than this cannot fitly be expected from me; and especially it cannot reasonably be expected, that I shall enter into an explanation upon a basis so vague as that which you have adopted. I trust, on more reflection, you will see the matter in the same light with me. If not, I can only regret the circumstance, and must abide the consequences.

The publication of Doctor Cooper was never seen by me till after the receipt of your letter.

I have the honor to be

Sir

Your obed. serv[t]

A Hamilton

Aaron Burr Esqr

Alexander Hamilton, 1802, by John Trumbull.
Courtesy of The New-York Historical Society, New York City.

William P. Van Ness's Account of the Events of June 21–22, 1804[1]

On the morning of Thursday the 21st I delivered to Col: Burr the above letter[2] and in the evening was furnished with the following letter for Genl Hamilton which I delivered to him at 12 o clock on friday the 22d Inst, (Mr B's letter 21 June) of which No. 3[3] is a copy.

1. "Van Ness's Narrative," AD, New York State Historical Association, Cooperstown, N.Y.

"The Draft of Van Ness's Narrative" at this point is essentially the same as the "Narrative."

2. Hamilton to Burr, June 20, 1804.

3. Burr to Hamilton, June 21, 1804.

Aaron Burr to Alexander Hamilton[1]

N York 21 June 1804

Sir

Your letter of the 20th inst. has been this day received. Having Considered it attentively I regret to find in it nothing of that sincerity and delicacy which you profess to Value.

Political opposition can never absolve Gentlemen from the Necessity of a rigid adherence to the laws of honor and the rules of decorum. I neither claim such priviledge nor indulge it in others.

The Common sense of Mankind affixes to the epithet adopted by Dr Cooper the idea of dishonor: it has been publicly applied to me under the sanction of your Name. The question is not whether he

---

1. ALS, New-York Historical Society; also ADfS, in the writing of Burr, New York State Historical Association, Cooperstown, N.Y. There is, in addition, an ADf, in the writing of Van Ness, New York State Historical Association.

The wording of the Burr draft is the same as the letter sent. The Van Ness draft, which differs in several particulars from the letter sent, reads as follows:

> I have this day received your letter of the 20th. Political opposition can never absolve gentlemen from a rigid adherence to the laws of honor or the rules of decorum. I neither claim such privelege myself nor indulge it in others.
>
> You appear sensible that from the style of your conversations inferences injurious to my character may have been drawn. I also feel a conviction that they have. Ordinary attention to the transactions of Society and the language of the world would evince that opinions highly desreputable to me have been expressed by you. Justified by these circumstances and peculiarly

has understood the Meaning of the word or has used it according to syntax and with grammatical accuracy, but whether you have authorised their application either directly or by uttering expressions or opinions derogatory to my honor. The time "when" is in your own knowledge, but no way material to me, as the Calumny has now first been

---

urged by the formal declaration of Mr Cooper respect for my own character & the opinion of the public demand the enquiry I have made. I cannot conceive it incumbent on me to trace reports publicly and extensively diffused to their source. They exist and can only be contradicted by a direct application to you. They are either well or ill founded which you alone can know, and a refusal to disavow them is not only confirmation of their truth but an adoption of the sentiments ascribed to you.

If you have used language of a dubious import without intending to convey injurious impressions, it behoves you as a man "of sincerity and delicacy" by a general disavowal of such intention to correct the hasty opinions of others and remove imputations which have thus been improperly connected with my reputation.

To the word "despicable" the common sense of Mankind, unaided by either Syntax or Grammar affixes the idea of *dishonor,* every shade of which demands investigation. The application of this term has been made under the sanction of your name. To ascertain how far it has been authorized by you is my object. Permit me therefore to solicit again your attention to the enquiry which I deemed before sufficiently intelligible, whether you have indulged in the use of language derogatory to my honor as a gentleman or which in this sense could warrant the expressions of Dr Cooper. To this I expect a definite reply, which must lead to an accomodation or to the only alternative which the circumstances of the case will justify.

disclosed so as to become the subject of my Notice, and as the effect is present and palpable.

Your letter has furnished me with new reasons for requiring a definite reply.

I have the honor to be

Sir

Your Obd[t] St

A. Burr

Gen[l] Hamilton

William P. Van Ness's Account of the Events of June 22, 1804[1]

General Hamilton perused it,[2] & said it was such a letter as he had hoped not to have received, that it contained several offensive expressions & seemed to close the door to all further reply, that he had hoped the answer he had returned to Col Burr's first letter would have given a different direction to the controversy, that he thought Mr Burr would have perceived that there was a difficulty in his making a more specific reply, & would have desired him to state what had fallen from him that might have given rise to the inference of Doctor Cooper. He would have done this frankly, & he believed it would not have been found to exceed the limits justifiable among political opponents. If Mr Burr should upon the suggestion of these ideas be disposed to give a different complexion to the discussion, he was willing to consider the last letter not delivered; but if that communication was not withdrawn he could make no reply and Mr Burr must pursue such course as he should deem most proper.

At the request of General Hamilton, I replied that I would detail these ideas to Col Burr; but added that if in his first letter he had introduced the idea (if it was a correct one) that he could recollect the use of no terms that would justify the construction made by Dr Cooper it would in my opin-

1. "Van Ness's Narrative," AD, New York State Historical Association, Cooperstown, N.Y.

"Draft of Van Ness's Narrative" differs from the "Narrative" at this point only in minor changes in wording.

2. Burr to Hamilton, June 21, 1804.

ion have opened a door for accomodation. General Hamilton then repeated the same objections to this measure which were stated in substance in his first letter to Col Burr.

When I was about leaving him he observed that if I preferred it, he would commit his refusal to writing. I replied that if he had resolved not to answer Col. Burr's letter, that I could report that to him verbally, without giving him the trouble of writing it. When he again repeated his determination not to answer, and that Col: Burr must pursue such course as he should deem most proper.

In the afternoon of this day I reported to Col: Burr at his house out of town the above answer and determination of General Hamilton.

Nathaniel Pendleton's Account of the Events of June 22, 1804[1]

On Saturday the 22d of June, General Hamilton, for the first time called on Mr. P. and communicated to him the preceding correspondence.[2] He informed him that in a conversation with Mr. V. N. at the time of receiving the last letter,[3] he told Mr. V. N. that he considered that letter as rude and offensive. And that it was not possible for him to give it any other answer than that Mr. Burr must take such steps as he might think proper. He said far-

1. *New-York Evening Post,* July 16, 1804.

This account of the conference was part of a longer narrative, prepared by Nathaniel Pendleton and printed in the *New-York Evening Post,* of the events and correspondence preceding the duel between Hamilton and Burr. This narrative as it appeared in the *New-York Evening Post* was preceded by the following statement:

> THE shocking catastrophe which has recently occurred, terminating the life of ALEXANDER HAMILTON, and which has spread a gloom over our city that will not be speedily dissipated, demands that the circumstances which led to it, or were intimately connected with it, should not be concealed from the world. When they shall be truly and fairly disclosed, however some may question the soundness of his Judgment on this occasion, all must be ready to do justice to the purity of his views, and the nobleness of his nature. It will only here be added, that the authenticity of the documents and the accuracy of the information which we have at last obtained, are beyond any question; and must put an end to all mistake or misrepresentation.

> The following is the correspondence that passed between General Hamilton, and Colonel Burr, together with an explanation of the conduct, motives

ther, that Mr. V. N. requested him to take time to deliberate, and then return an answer, when he might possibly entertain a different opinion, and that he would call on him to receive it. That his reply to Mr. V. N. was, that he did not perceive it possible for him to give any other answer than that he had mentioned, unless Mr. Burr would take back his last letter and write one which would admit of a different reply. He then gave Mr. P. the letter hereafter mentioned of the 23d[4] of June, to be delivered to Mr. V. N. when he should call on Mr. P. for an answer, and went to his country house.

The next day General Hamilton received, while there, the following letter.[5]

------

and views of General Hamilton, written with his own hand the evening before the meeting took place and only to have been seen in the deplorable event that followed.

Pendleton, who had been born in Virginia, was a veteran of the Revolution. After the war he practiced law in Georgia and was a delegate to the Constitutional Convention. He settled in New York City in 1796 and soon became a prominent lawyer in that city. He was Hamilton's second in the duel with Burr.

2. The correspondence here referred to is that which precedes this statement in the *New-York Evening Post* (Burr to Hamilton, June 18, 1804; Hamilton to Burr, June 20, 1804; Burr to Hamilton, June 21, 1804).

3. Burr to Hamilton, June 21, 1804.

4. This is a mistake, for the letter Hamilton sent to Burr was actually dated June 22, 1804. This letter was not delivered until June 25, 1804.

5. Van Ness to Hamilton, June 23, 1804.

Alexander Hamilton to Aaron Burr[1]

New York June 22^d 1804

Sir

Your first letter,[2] in a style too peremptory, made a demand, in my opinion, unprecedented and unwarrantable. My answer, pointing out the embarrassment, gave you an opportunity to take a less exceptionable course. You have not chosen to do it, but by your last letter,[3] received this day, containing expressions indecorous[4] and improper, you have increased the difficulties to explanation, intrinsically incident to the nature of your application.

If by a "definite reply" you mean the direct avowal or disavowal required in your first letter, I have no other answer to give than that which has already been given. If you mean any thing differ-

1. ALS, New York State Historical Association, Cooperstown, N.Y.; also ADf, New-York Historical Society.

This letter was given by Hamilton to Pendleton, who did not deliver it until June 25, 1804.

2. Burr to Hamilton, June 18, 1804.

3. Burr to Hamilton, June 21, 1804.

4. In the draft, Hamilton first wrote and then crossed out the word "rude."

5. In the draft, Hamilton originally wrote for his final paragraph: "I have no other reply to make than that it remains for you to take such measures as shall appear to you expedient." Hamilton then crossed out these words and added the paragraph that appears in the final version sent to Burr.

In a note on the draft, Hamilton wrote: "This clause [the final paragraph in version sent to Burr] and word indecorous substituted with the advice of M^r P——."

ent admitting of greater latitude, it is requisite you should explain.[5]

> I have the honor to be
> Sir   Your obed Serv[t]
> A Hamilton

Aaron Burr Esqr

William P. Van Ness's Account of the Events of June 22–23, 1804[1]

In the afternoon of this day[2] I reported to Col: Burr at his house out of town the above answer[3] and determination of General Hamilton and promised to call on him again in the evening to learn his further wishes. I was detained in Town however this evening by some private business and did not call on Col: Burr untill the following morning Saturday the 23[d] Inst: I then received from him a letter for Genl Hamilton which is numbered 4,[4] but as will presently be explained never was delivered. The substance of it will be found in N[o] 12.[5]

1. "Van Ness's Narrative," AD, New York State Historical Association, Cooperstown, N.Y.

At this point the "Draft of Van Ness's Narrative" reads as follows:

> In the afternoon of this day I reported to Col B at his house out of town the above conversation, and promised to call on him again in the evening for his further instructions. I was detained in town this evening by some private business, and did not call on Col: Burr according to appointment.
>
> On Saturday morning the 23[d]. I went out to his house, and received from him for Genl. Hamilton a letter of which N[o] 4 [Burr to Hamilton, June 22, 1804] is a copy with some instructions for a verbal communication of which N[o] 5 ["Aaron Burr's Instructions to William P. Van Ness for a Verbal Communication to Alexander Hamilton," June 22, 1804] is a copy.

2. June 22, 1804.

3. This refers to the conversation between Hamilton and Van Ness as recorded in "William P. Van Ness's Account of the Events of June 22, 1804."

4. Burr to Hamilton, June 22, 1804.

5. Van Ness to Pendleton, June 27, 1804.

Aaron Burr to Alexander Hamilton[1]

N York June 22^d. 1804

Sir

M^r V Ness has this evening reported to me verbally that you refuse to answer my last letter,[2] that you consider the course I have taken as intemperate and unnecessary and some other conversation which it is improper that I should notice.

My request to you was in the first instance prepared in a form the most simple in order that you might give to the affair that course to which you might be induced by your temper and your knowledge of facts. I relied with unsuspecting faith that from the frankness of a soldier and the Candor of a gentleman I might expect an ingeneous declaration; that if, as I had reason to believe, you had used expressions derogatory to my honor, you would have had the Spirit to Maintain or the Magnaminity to retract them, and, that if from your language injurious inferences had been improperly drawn, Sincerity and decency would have pointed out to you the propriety of correcting errors which might thus have been widely diffused.

With these impressions, I was greatly disappointed in receiving from you a letter[3] which I

1. ALS, from a facsimile in the Library of Congress.

On June 25, 1804, Van Ness called on Hamilton to deliver this letter, but he did not do so as Hamilton presented him with a reply to Burr's letter of June 21, 1804. In his "Narrative," Van Ness states that this letter (Burr to Hamilton, June 22, 1804) was never delivered ("William P. Van Ness's Account of the Events of June 22–23, 1804").

2. Burr to Hamilton, June 21, 1804.

could only consider as evasive and which in manner, is not altogether decorous. In one expectation however, I was not wholly deceived, for at the close of your letter I find an intimation, that if I should dislike your refusal to acknowledge or deny the charge, you were ready to meet the consequences. This I deemed a sort of defiance, and I should have been justified if I had chosen to make it the basis of an immediate Message: Yet, as you had also said something (though in my opinion unfounded) of the indefiniteness of my request; as I believed that your communication was the offspring, rather of false pride than of reflection, and, as I felt the utmost reluctance to proceed to extremities while any other hope remained, my request was repeated in terms more definite. To this you refuse all reply, reposing, as I am bound to presume on the tender of an alternative insinuated in your letter.

Thus, Sir, you have invited the course I am about [to] pursue, and now by your silence impose it upon me. [If] therefore your determinations are final, of which I am not permitted to doubt M^r. Van Ness is authorised to communicate my further expectations either to yourself or to such friend as you may be pleased to indicate.

> I have the honor to be
> Your Ob st
> A. Burr

3. Hamilton to Burr, June 20, 1804.

Aaron Burr's Instructions to William P. Van Ness for a Verbal Communication to Alexander Hamilton[1]

[New York, June 22, 1804][2]

A. B. Far from conceiving that rivalship authorises a latitude not otherwise justifiable, always feels greater delicacy in such cases, and would think it meanness to speak of a rival but in terms of respect; to do justice to his merits; to be silent of his foibles. Such has invariably been his conduct toward Jay, Adams, and Hamilton; the only three who can be supposed to have stood in that relation to him.

That he has too much reason to believe that in regard of Mr. Hamilton, there has been no reciprocity; for several years his name has been lent to the support of base slanders. He has never had the generosity, the magnanimity, or the candor to contradict or disavow. B forbears to particularize as it could only tend to produce new irritations; but having made great sacrifices for the sake of harmony, having exercised forbearance till it approached to humiliation, he has seen no effect pro-

1. New York *Morning Chronicle,* July 17, 1804.

2. In the "Draft of Van Ness's Narrative" Van Ness states that these notes were handed to him at the same time as the letter of June 22, 1804: "On Saturday morning the 23[d] I went out to his house, and received from him for Genl Hamilton a letter of which N° 4 [Burr to Hamilton, June 22, 1804] is a Copy with some instructions for a verbal communication."

These "Instructions" are again referred to in "William P. Van Ness's Account of the Events of June 25, 1804."

duced by such conduct, but a repetition of injury. He is obliged to conclude that there is, on the part of Mr. Hamilton, a settled and implacable malevolence; that he will never cease in his conduct towards Mr B to violate those courtesies of life, and that, hence, he has no alternative but to announce these things to the world, which consistently with Mr. B's ideas of propriety, can be done in no way but that which he has adopted. He is incapable of revenge, still less is he capable of imitating the conduct of Mr. Hamilton, by committing secret depredations on his fame and character; but these things must have an end.

William P. Van Ness's Account of the Events of June 23, 1804[1]

When I returned With this letter[2] to the City which was about 2 O clock in the afternoon of the same day,[3] I sent a Note to Genl Hamilton's Office and also to his house[4] desiring to know when it would be convenient for him to receive a communication. The Servant as he informed me received for answer at both places that Genl Hamilton had left the City and was gone to his Country residence. I then wrote a Note to Genl Hamilton of which N° 5[5] is a Copy & sent it out to him in the Country.

1. "Van Ness's Narrative," AD, New York State Historical Association, Cooperstown, N.Y.

The "Draft of Van Ness's Narrative" is essentially the same as his "Narrative" at this point.

2. Burr to Hamilton, June 22, 1804.

3. June 23, 1804.

4. The two notes here referred to have not been found.

5. Van Ness to Hamilton, June 23, 1804.

William P. Van Ness to
Alexander Hamilton[1]

[New York] June 23, 1804

Sir

In the afternoon of yesterday I reported to Col. Burr the result of my last interview with you, and appointed the evening to receive his further instructions. Some private engagements however prevented me from calling on him 'till this morning. On my return to the City I found upon enquiry both at your office and house, that you had returned to your residence in the Country. Least an interview there might be less agreeable to you than elsewhere, I have taken the liberty of addressing you this note, to enquire when and where it will be most convenient to you to receive a communication

Your most & very hum Sert.
W: P: Van Ness

Genl Hamilton

1. ALS, New-York Historical Society; also ADfS, New York State Historical Association, Cooperstown, N.Y.

Nathaniel Pendleton's Account of
the Events of June 23, 1804[1]

Mr. P—— understood from General Hamilton that he immediately answered,[2] that if the communication was pressing he would receive it at his country house that day, if not, he would be at his house in town the next morning at nine o'clock. But he did not give Mr. P. any copy of this note.

1. *New-York Evening Post,* July 16, 1804.
2. Hamilton to Van Ness, June 23, 1804.

Alexander Hamilton to
William P. Van Ness[1]

Grange[2] June 23. 1804

Sir

I was in Town to day till half past one. I thank you for the delicacy which dictated your note to me. If it is indispensable the communication should be made before Monday Morning, I must receive it here. But I should think this cannot be important. On monday by Nine I shall be in Town at my house in Cæder Street N⁰ 52, where I should be glad to see you. An additional reason for preferring this is, that I am unwilling to occasion to you trouble.

With esteem I am Sir
Your obed ser
AH

Wᵐ P. Van Ness Esqr.

1. ALS, New York State Historical Association, Cooperstown, N.Y.

2. This was the name of Hamilton's country home, which was located between what are now 141st and 145th streets on the west side of Manhattan Island.

Nathaniel Pendleton's Account of the Events of June 23–25, 1804[1]

This letter,[2] although dated on the 23d June,[3] remained in Mr. P.'s possession until the 25th, within which period he had several conversations with Mr. V. N. In these conversations Mr. P. endeavored to illustrate and enforce the propriety of the ground which General Hamilton had taken. Mr. P. mentioned to Mr. V. N. as the result, that if Col. Burr would write a letter, requesting to know in substance whether in the conversation to which Dr. Cooper alluded, any particular instance of dishonorable conduct was imputed to Col. Burr, or whether there was any impeachment of his private character, Gen. Hamilton would declare to the best of his recollection what passed in that conversation; and Mr. P. read to Mr. V. N. a paper containing the substance of what Gen. H. would say on that subject, which is as follows:[4]

1. *New-York Evening Post,* July 16, 1804.

2. Hamilton to Burr, June 22, 1804.

3. This is an error, for as indicated in note 2, the letter was dated June 22.

4. See next document.

Nathaniel Pendleton's First Report of the Remarks Made by Alexander Hamilton in the Presence of Dr. Charles Cooper[1]

[New York, June 25, 1804][2]

General Hamilton says he cannot imagine to what Doct^r Cooper may have alluded unless it were to a conversation at Mr Taylors in Albany last winter, (at which Mr Taylor he & General H—— were present) Genl H—— cannot recollect distinctly the particulars of that conversation so as to undertake to repeat them, without running the risk of varying or omitting what might be deemed important circumstances. The expressions are intirely forgotten, and the Specific ideas imperfectly remembered; but to the best of his recollection it consisted of comments on the political principles and views of Col. Burr, and the results that might be expected from them in the event of his Election as Governor, without referrence to any particular instance of past conduct, or to private character.

1. AD, in writing of Pendleton, New-York Historical Society.

This statement was presumably dictated by Hamilton.

2. See "Nathaniel Pendleton's Account of the Events of June 23–25, 1804" for the dating of this document.

William P. Van Ness's Account of the Events of June 25, 1804[1]

At nine O clock on Monday the 25th Inst: I called on Genl Hamilton at his house in Cedar Street to present the letter N⁰ 4[2] already alluded to, and with instructions for a verbal communication of which the following Notes N⁰ 7[3] handed me by M[r] Burr were to be the basis. The substance of which though in terms as much softened as my instructions would permit, was accordingly communicated to Genl Hamilton.

1. "Van Ness's Narrative," AD, New York State Historical Association, Cooperstown, N.Y.

The "Draft of Van Ness's Narrative" differs from his "Narrative" in only insignificant respects at this point.

2. Burr to Hamilton, June 22, 1804. This letter was never delivered ("William P. Van Ness's Account of the Events of June 22–23, 1804").

3. See "Aaron Burr's Instructions to William P. Van Ness for a Verbal Communication to Alexander Hamilton," June 22, 1804.

William P. Van Ness's Further Account of the Events of June 25, 1804[1]

Before I delivered the written communication with which I was charged Genl Hamilton said that he had prepared a written reply[2] to Col: Burr's letter of the 21st which he had left with Mr xxx[3] and wished me to receive. I answered that the communication I had to make to him was predicated upon the idea that he would make no reply to Mr Burrs letter of the 21st Inst: and that I had so understood

1. "Van Ness's Narrative," AD, New York State Historical Association, Cooperstown, N.Y.

In the draft of his "Narrative," Van Ness wrote:

I called on Genl Hamilton at his house in Cedar Street to deliver the letter Nº 4 [Burr to Hamilton, June 22, 1804], and make the remarks I was instructed to do. When I entered he said before I delivered any communication he wished to state that he had prepared a written reply [Hamilton to Burr, June 22, 1804] to Mr Burr's last letter, which was in the hands of Mr Pendleton who would deliver it to me. I answered that the communication I had to make to him was predicated upon the idea that he would make no reply to Mr Burr's letter of the 21st Instant. And that I had so understood him in our conversation of the 22d Inst: Genl. Hamilton said that he believed he had offered to give a written reply which was however omitted, I said I recollected when he answered verbally that he could not answer Mr Burr's letter that he offered to put *that* in writing, and I concluded by observing that if he wished to reply that I would receive it. In our conversation I repeated to him as nearly as I could recollect the observations contained in Nº. 5 ["Aaron Burr's Instructions to William P. Van Ness for a Verbal Communication to Alexander Hamilton," June 22, 1804]. Genl Hamilton said that he

him in our conversation of the 22^d. Genl H said that he believed before I left him, he had offered to give a written reply. I observed that when he answered verbally he had offered to put that *refusal* in writing but that if he had now prepared a written reply I would receive it with pleasure. I accordingly called on M^r xxx on the same day Monday June 25 between 1 & 2 o clock P M, and stated to him the result of my recent interview with Genl Hamilton, and the reference he had made to him.

I then received from M^r xxx the letter N° 8. . . .[4]

This letter was unsealed, but I did not read it

---

disclaimed every idea of personal enmity. That to be sure he had been a uniform political opponent of Col. Burr, but in that opposition he had been governed by public principles. Between 1 & 2 O clock on the same day Monday 25 June I called on Mr Pendleton and stated that after my interview with Genl H. on friday, I had reported to Col B that Genl H would make no reply to his letter of the 21 that I then received from Col B. a communication for Genl H; predicated upon that reply, that agreeable to appt I had seen Genl H. at 9 O clock, & that he supposed I had somewhat misunderstood him, and wished me to call on his Mr P. for a written reply which had been left with him. I then received from Mr Pendleton the letter N° 8, but first premised that we were averse to continuing this correspondence any longer and that we should only return a verbal answer whether it was satisfactory or not. It was unsealed but I did not read it in his presence. After some little conversation concerning what Genl: Hamilton would say upon the subject of the present controversy, Mr Pendleton left me for the purpose of seeing and consulting Mr Hamilton.

2. Hamilton to Burr, June 22, 1804.

3. Pendleton.

4. Hamilton to Burr, June 22, 1804.

in his presence. After some conversation relative to what Genl. Hamilton would say on the subject of the present controversy, during which M^r xxx read from a paper[5] his ideas on the subject, he left me for the purpose of seeing and consulting Mr Hamilton taking the paper with him.

5. This paper was probably "Nathaniel Pendleton's First Report of the Remarks Made by Alexander Hamilton in the Presence of Dr. Charles Cooper," June 25, 1804.

Nathaniel Pendleton's Account of the Events of June 25, 1804[1]

After the delivery of the letter of the 23d,[2] as above mentioned: in another interview with Mr. V. N. he desired Mr. P. to give him *in writing* the substance of what he had proposed on the part of General Hamilton, which Mr. P. did in the words following—[3]

1. *New-York Evening Post,* July 16, 1804.

2. Date on the manuscript of this letter from Hamilton to Burr is June 22, 1804.

3. See next document.

Nathaniel Pendleton's Second Report of Remarks Made by Alexander Hamilton in the Presence of Dr. Charles Cooper[1]

[New York, June 25, 1804][2]

In answer to a letter, properly adapted to obtain from Gen[l]. Hamilton a declaration whether he had charged Col. B. with any particular instance of dishonorable conduct, or had impeached his private character, either in the conversation alluded to by Doctor Cooper or any other particular instance, to be specified.

He would be able to answer consistently with his honor, and the truth in substance, That the conversation to which Doctor Cooper alluded, turned wholly on political topics, and did not attribute to Col[o] Burr, any instance of dishonorable conduct, nor relate to his private character, and in relation to any other language or conversation of Gen[l]. H. which Col[o]. B will specify; a prompt & frank avowal or denial will be given.

1. AD, in the writing of Pendleton, New York State Historical Association, Cooperstown, N.Y.; also AD, in the writing of Pendleton, New-York Historical Society.

2. See "Nathaniel Pendleton's Account of the Events of June 25, 1804" for the dating of this document.

Continuation of William P. Van Ness's Further Account of the Events of June 25, 1804[1]

In about an hour[2] he[3] called at my house. I informed him, that I had shewn to Col Burr the letter[4] that in his opinion it amounted to nothing more than the verbal reply I had already reported, that it left the business precisely were it then was,

1. "Van Ness's Narrative," AD, New York State Historical Association, Cooperstown, N.Y.

The "Draft of Van Ness's Narrative" reads as follows:

> At ½ past 2 oclock Mr Pendleton called at my house. I told him that I had perused the letter [Hamilton to Burr, June 22, 1804] which he had given me a short time before and shewn it also to Col: Burr. That it appeared to Col Burr to be nothing more than the verbal reply which I had already reported to him. That it left the business precisely were it was then. That I did not think it proper or necessary to ask now for further explanation from us. That Mr Burr had very explicitly stated the injuries he had received and the satisfaction he required. He then presented me with a paper ["Nathaniel Pendleton's First Report of the Remarks Made by Alexander Hamilton in the Presence of Dr. Charles Cooper," June 25, 1804] to which I objected as being confined to a particular occasion, that we required a Genl disavowal of any intention on the part of Mr Hamilton in his various conversations to convey impressions derogatory to the honor of Mr Burr. Mr Pendleton replied that he believed Genl Hamilton would have no objection to say that much and left me for the purpose of consulting Genl. H, and wished me to call on him in the course of the afternoon for an answer.

2. In midafternoon.

that Mr Burr had very explicitly stated the injuries he had received and the reparation he demanded, and that he did not think it proper to be asked now for further explanations. Toward the conclusion of our conversation I informed him that Col: Burr required a General disavowal of any intention on the part of Genl Hamilton in his various conversations to convey impressions derogatory to the honor of Mr Burr. M^r. xxx^5 replied that he believed Genl Hamilton would have no objection to make such declaration and left me for the purpose of consulting him requesting me to call in the course of the afternoon for an answer. I called on him accordingly about 6. O clock. He then observed that Genl Hamilton declined making such a disavowal as I had stated in our last conversation, that he M^r xxx did not then perceive the whole force and extent of it, and presented me with the following paper N° 9^6 which I transmitted in the evening to M^r. Burr

3. Pendleton.

4. Hamilton to Burr, June 22, 1804.

5. Pendleton.

6. "Nathaniel Pendleton's Second Report of Remarks Made by Alexander Hamilton in the Presence of Dr. Charles Cooper," June 25, 1804.

Aaron Burr to William P. Van Ness[1]

[New York, June 25, 1804]

I am disappointed of my ride.

If xxx[2] should propose to charge you with any verbal message, you may reply, that being authorised for a particular purpose, you cannot so far exceed your power and assume upon yourself as to present to your principal an overture for Negociation on a new basis — that you consider the Negociation in which you engaged, as concluded and that it would be highly improper in you to propose one anew as *his agent* — that if he should think proper to attempt any thing of the kind, it must be through some other channel.

If it should be asked whether there is no alternative, most certainly there is; but more will now be required than would have been asked at first.

These hints are only intended to attract your attention to the Various Shapes which the thing may assume so that you may be at all points prepared.

25 June

1. AD, in writing of Burr, New York State Historical Association, Cooperstown, N.Y.

2. Pendleton.

Statement Prepared by William P. Van Ness for Alexander Hamilton

[New York, June 25, 1804]

Being apprised that expressions are ascribed to me impeaching the honor and affecting the private reputation of Col. Burr, and perceiving that reports to this effect have been widely disseminated, I feel it due to my own honor, as also to that of a gentleman thus traduced under the sanction of my name, to remove such injurious impressions —

I therefore frankly and explicitly disclaim and disavow the use of any expressions tending to impeach the honor of Col. Burr. My own sincerity and candor require this declaration; and, while I regret that my expressions have been misrepresented or miscontrued, I can only account for the inferences which have been drawn, from them, by supposing that language I may have employed in the warmth of political discourse has been represented in a lattitude entirely foreign from my sentiments or my wishes.

1. AD, in writing of Van Ness, New York State Historical Association, Cooperstown, N.Y.

Statement Prepared by Aaron Burr
for Alexander Hamilton[1]

[New York, June 25, 1804]

G H being apprised that expressions are ascribed to him impeaching the honor & affecting the private reputation of A B and perceiving that reports to this effect have been widely disseminated feels it due to his own honor as also to that of a gentleman thus traduced under the sanction of his name, to remove all such injurious impressions.

G H frankly & explicitly disclaims & disavows the use of any expressions tending to impeach the honor of A. B. He feels the sincerity & candor of his own character injured by a charge of the kind, & while he regrets that his expressions have been misrepresented or misconstrued, he can only account for this effect by supposing that language he may have employed in the warmth of political discourse has been understood, or represented in a latitude entirely foreign from his sentiments or his wishes.

If G H has on any occasions uttered such expressions he feels a propriety in fully & explicitly with drawing them as the ebulitions of party feeling which may have escaped him in the heat of political discourse but which he is conscious are unmerited & regrets having employed.

1. AD, in writing of Burr, New York State Historical Association, Cooperstown, N.Y.

Nyork 21 June 1804

Sir

Your letter of the 20th inst. has been this day received. Having considered it attentively I regret to find in it nothing of that sincerity and delicacy which you profess to value.

Political opposition can never absolve Gentlemen from the necessity of a rigid adherence to the laws of honor and the rules of decorum. I neither claim such priviledge nor indulge it in others.

The common sense of mankind affixes to the epithet adopted by Dr Cooper the idea of dishonor: it has been publicly applied to me under the sanction of your name. The question is not whether he has understood the meaning of the word or has used it according to Syntax and grammatical accuracy, but whether you have authorised this application either directly or by utturing expressions or opinions derogatory to my honor. The time "when" is in your own knowledge, but no way material to me, as the calumny has now first been disclosed so as to become the subject of my notice, and as the effect is present and palpable.

Your letter has furnished me with new reasons for requiring a definite reply.

I have the honor to be

Sir

your Obt St
A Burr

Genl Hamilton

Letter of Burr to Hamilton, June 21, 1804.
Courtesy of The New-York Historical Society, New York City.

Aaron Burr to William P. Van Ness[1]

[New York, June 26, 1804]

The last prop^n. of Genl H. is a worse libel then even the letter of D^r C & throughout manifests a disposition to evade.

A "letter properly adapted"[2] — who is to judge of this — Mr B. will judge for himself & thinks his two letters very properly adapted & having expressed himself definitively on that point he is surprized to find it again brought in question.

"Any particular instance of dishonorable Conduct"[3] This seems intended to leave ample Room for the inference that there have been general opinions and general charges.

"in relation to any other language &c" which "Col. B. shall *specify*"[4] — Col. B. is ignorant of the particular Conversations & expressions which Genl H. may have had or used & he will only inquire from Genl. H. himself. That he has said things derogatory to M^r B's honor is to be presumed from the letter of Dr C. until it shall be contradicted by Genl. H.

If Mr B. should specify & Genl. H. should deny as to one particular Conversation, Dr C. & the world may say "true, but the day anterior or the day subsequent, such things were said by Genl. H."

1. AD, in writing of Burr, New York State Historical Association, Cooperstown, N.Y.

2. This quotation is from "Nathaniel Pendleton's Second Report of Remarks Made by Alexander Hamilton in the Presence of Dr. Charles Cooper," June 25, 1804.

3. *Ibid.*

4. *Ibid.*

and this would indeed be a fair inference from such partial negation. These things must be perfectly obvious to the perspicatious mind of Gen¹ H. Propositions therefore fraught with such ambiguity and liable to such injurious Construction must be considered as insidious and insulting and they call imperiously for the last appeal.

I was writing the preceeding by way of notes for you when your boy arrived. They are sent to you unfinished. It seems that our sentiments are pretty much in harmony. Interweave into your's what you think proper of the preceeding. I will be at your house before noon & will dine with you.

[June] 26

William P. Van Ness's Account of the Events of June 26, 1804[1]

The following day (Tuesday 26. June) as early as was convenient I had an interview with Col: Burr, who informed me that he considered Gen[l] Hamiltons proposition a mere evasion, which evinced a desire to leave the injurious impressions which had arisen from the conversations of Gen[l] Hamilton in full force. That when he had undertaken to investigate an injury his honor had sustained it would be unworthy of him not to make that investigation complete. He gave me further instructions which are substantially contained in the following letter to M[r]. xxx[2] N[o] 10[3]

1. "Van Ness's Narrative," AD, New York State Historical Association, Cooperstown, N.Y.

At this point, the "Draft of Van Ness's Narrative" is substantially the same as the "Narrative."

2. Pendleton.

3. Van Ness to Pendleton, June 26, 1804.

William P. Van Ness to
Nathaniel Pendleton[1]

[New York, June 26, 1804]

Sir

The letter[2] which you yesterday delivered me and your subsequent communications,[3] in Col Burrs opinion evince no disposition on the part of Gen[l] Hamilton to come to a satisfactory accomodation. The injury complained of and the reparation expected are so definitely expressed in Col. Burr's letter of the 21st Instant that there is not perceived a necessity for further explanation on his part. The

1. ALS, New-York Historical Society; also two drafts in Van Ness's writing and a partial draft in Burr's writing. These three drafts are in New York State Historical Association, Cooperstown, N.Y.

The first draft of this letter, which is in Van Ness's writing, reads as follows:

The letter which you yesterday delivered me from Gen[l] Hamilton in Col. Burr's opinion evinces as little disposition on the part of Gen[l] Hamilton to come to a satisfactory accomodation <as any of his former communications & least it may not be accurately understood however what Col. Burr conceives to be the injury he has sustained, and the reparation which he deems necessary, permit me again to solicit your attention to his letter of the 21 Instant. You will there find his complaint specified in language so definite and precise as to preclude in his opinion the necessity of all further explanation on his part. It is impossible for Col. Burr to point out the various objectionable conversations and expressions which at different times may have been indulged in by Gen[l] Hamilton, and from him alone he can make the enquiry. It is too evident to be denied, that reports injurious to the char-

difficulty that would result from confining the enquiry to any particular times and occasions must be manifest. The denial of a specified conversation only, would leave strong implications that on other occasions improper language had been used. When and where injurious opinions and expressions have been uttered by Gen¹ Hamilton must be best known to him and of him only will Col. Burr enquire. No denial or declaration will be satisfactory unless it be general, so as wholly to exclude the idea that rumors derogatory to Col. Burr's honor have originated with Gen¹. Hamilton or have been *fairly* inferred from any thing he has said. A definite reply to a requisition of this nature was demanded by Col: Burrs letter of the 21 Inst: This being refused invites the alternative alluded to in Gen¹ Hamilton's letter of the 20ᵗʰ. It was required by the posi-

---

acter of Col. Burr have been extensively circulated under the sanction of Gen¹ Hamilton's name, and that language derogatory to his honor has been used by Gen¹ Hamilton he has sufficient reason to presume. The time when is not material, and you must perceive the difficulty that would result from a specification. Should Gen¹ Hamilton deny having used exceptionable language on any specified occasion, this though true would not remedy the evil which is complained of, for the preceeding or subsequent day might be referred to as that on which the injury had been done and the controversy would thus become endless. A retraction or *denial* therefore of all such declarations *or a disavowal of any intention to impeach the character of Col Burr without reference* to time or place is the only reparation that can be made,> and a definite reply to a requisition of this nature is demanded in Col: Burr's letter of the 21ˢᵗ Inst. This being refused; invites the alternative alluded to, in Genl Hamiltons

tion in which the controversy was placed by Gen¹ Hamilton on friday last and I was immediately furnished with a communication demanding a personal interview. The necessity of this measure has not in the opinion of Col Burr been diminished by the General's last letter or any communication which has since been received.

I am consequently again instructed to deliver you a message as soon as it may be convenient for you to receive it. I beg therefore you will be so

_____

letter of the [20] inst. It was demanded by the position in which the controversy was placed by Gen¹ Hamilton on the 22ᵈ Inst. and I was immediately furnished with a communication demanding *the usual* interview. The necessity of resorting to this measure has not in the opinion of Col: Burr been diminished by Gen¹ Hamiltons last letter or any subsequent communications which have been received and I am again instructed to deliver you a Message as soon as it may be convenient for you to receive it. If therefore you will have the politeness to inform me at what hour I shall wait on you, I shall be greatly obliged.

This draft is endorsed in Van Ness's writing as follows:

Dʳᵗ letter 1ˢᵗ to Mʳ Pendleton which was altered by Col B and not sent — this be substituted.

The following fragmentary draft in Burr's writing was used as a substitute for the portion of the first draft that appears within the < >:

The injury complained of and the reparation expected, are so definitely expressed in his letter of the 21 that there is not perceived a necessity for further explanation on his part — to ask of him to specify particular times & occasions is *absurd* — The denial of a specified conversation only, would have strong impli-

good as to inform me at what hour I can have the pleasure of seeing you.

Your Most obt &
Very hum Sert
W: P: Van Ness

June 26, 1804
Nathaniel Pendleton Esq[r].

———

cations that on other occasions [word omitted] language had been used

When and where injurious expressions and opinions have been [word omitted] is best known to Gen[l] H & of him only will Col. B. inquire. No denial or declaration will be satisfactory unless it be general so as perfectly to exclude the idea that rumors derogatory to Col. B. honor can have originated with Gen[l] H or have been fairly inferred from any thing he had said.

The final draft in Van Ness's writing and signed by him is almost identical with the letter sent.

2. Hamilton to Burr, June 22, 1804.

3. This probably refers to Pendleton's first and second reports of "Remarks Made by Alexander Hamilton in the Presence of Dr. Charles Cooper," June 25, 1804.

Nathaniel Pendleton to
William P. Van Ness[1]

[New York] 26 june 1804

Sir

I have communicated to General Hamilton the letter you did me the honor to write me of this date. The expectations now disclosed as on the part of Col°. Burr, appear to him to have greatly changed and extended the original ground of inquiry, and instead of presenting a particular and definite case for explanation, seem to aim at nothing less than an inquisition into his most confidential, as well as other conversations through the whole period of his acquaintance with Col Burr. While he was prepared to meet the particular case fully and fairly he thinks it inadmissible that he should be expected to answer at large as to any thing that he may possibly have said in relation to the character of Col°. Burr, at any time or upon any occasion. Though he is not conscious that any charges that are in circulation to the prejudice of Col. Burr have Originated with him, except one which may have been so considered, and which has been long since explained between Col. Burr and himself; yet he cannot consent to be questioned generally as to any *rumours* which may be afloat

1. ALS, New York State Historical Association, Cooperstown, N.Y.; also ADfS, in the writing of Hamilton, but signed by Pendleton, New-York Historical Society.

Van Ness's only comment on this letter was that he received it on the evening of June 26 and that he transmitted it to Burr ("Van Ness's Narrative," AD, New York State Historical Association).

derogatory to the character of Col°. Burr without specification of the particular rumours, many of them probably unknown to him. He does not however mean to authorise any conclusion as to the real nature of his Conduct in relation to Col. Burr, by his declining so loose and vague a basis of explanation; and he disavows an unwillingness to come to a satisfactory, provided it be an honorable accommodation. His objection is to the very indefinite ground which Col. Burr has assumed, in which he is sorry to be able to discover nothing short of predetermined hostility.

Presuming therefore that it will be adhered to he has instructed me to receive the message which you have it charge to deliver. For this purpose I shall be at home and at your command tomorrow morning from eight to ten oClock.

I have the honor be respectfully

Your Obedient Servt.

Nathl. Pendleton

William P. Van Ness Esqr.

William P. Van Ness to
Nathaniel Pendleton[1]

[New York, June 27, 1804]

Sir

The letter which I had the honor to receive from you under date of yesterday, states among other things, that in Genl Hamilton's opinion, Col: Burr has taken a very indefinite ground in which he evinces nothing short of predetermined hostility; and that Genl Hamilton thinks it inadmissable that the enquiry should extend to his confidential as well as other conversations. To this Col. Burr can only reply that secret whispers traducing his fame and impeaching his honor are at least equally injurious, with slanders publickly uttered; That Genl H. had at no time and in no place a right to use any such injurious expressions; and that the partial negative he is desposed to give with the reservations he wishes to make are proofs that he has done the injury specified.

Col: Burr's request was in the first instance proposed in a form the most simple, in order that Genl

1. ALS, New-York Historical Society; also ADf, in writing of Van Ness, New York State Historical Association, Cooperstown, N.Y.

In "Van Ness's Narrative" this letter is preceded by the following:

I transmitted this [Pendleton to Van Ness, June 26, 1804] to Col: Burr and after a conference with him in which I received his further instructions and that no misunderstanding might arise from verbal communications I committed to writing the remarks contained in N°. 12 which follows ("Van Ness's Narrative," AD, New York State Historical Association).

Hamilton might give to the affair that course to which he might be induced by his temper and his knowledge of facts. Col. B. trusted with confidence that from the frankness of a soldier and the candor of a gentleman he might expect an ingenuous declaration; that if, as he had reason to believe Gen¹ H. had used expressions derogatory to his honor, he would have had the magnanimity to retract them; and that if, from his language injurious inferences had been improperly drawn he would have perceived the propriety of correcting errors, which might thus have been widely diffused. With these impressions Col. Burr was greatly surprised at receiving a letter which he considered as evasive and which in manner he deemed not altogether decorous. In one expectation however, he was not wholly deceived, for the close of Gen¹ Hamilton's letter contained an intimation that if Col. Burr should dislike his refusal to acknowledge or deny, he was ready to meet the consequences. This Col. B. deemed a sort of defiance, and would have felt justified in making it the basis of an immediate message. But as the communication contained something concerning the indefiniteness of his request; as he believed it rather the offspring of false pride than of reflection, and as he felt the utmost reluctance to proceed to extremities, while any other hope remained, his request was repeated in terms more explicit. The replies and propositions on the part of Gen¹ H. have in Col. B's opinion been constantly in substance the same.

Col: Burr disavows all motives of predetermined hostility. A charge by which he thinks insult is added to injury, he feels as a gentleman should feel, when his honor is impeached or as-sailed, and without sensations of hostility or wishes of revenge, he is determined to vindicate that honor at such hazard as the nature of the case de-mands.

The length to which this correspondence has extended only tending to prove that the satisfactory redress, earnestly desired cannot be obtained, he deems it useless to offer any proposition except the simple Message which I shall now have the honor to deliver

I have the honor to be with great respect
Your obt & very hum Servt
W. P. Van Ness
Wednesday morning June 27, 1804

Alexander Hamilton's Remarks on his Impending Duel with Aaron Burr[1]

[New York, June 27–July 4, 1804]

On my expected interview with Col Burr, I think it proper to make some remarks explanatory of my conduct, motives and views.

I was certainly desirous of avoiding this interview, for the most cogent reasons —

1. My religious and moral principles are strongly opposed to the practice of Duelling and it would ever give me pain to be obliged to shed the blood of a fellow creature in a private combat forbidden by the laws.

2 My wife and Children are extremely dear to me, and my life is of the utmost importance to them, in various views.

3. I feel a sense of obligation towards my creditors; who in case of accident to me, by the forced sale of my property, may be in some degree sufferers. I did not think myself at liberty as a man of probity, lightly to expose them to this hazard.

4 I am conscious of no *ill-will* to Col Burr, dis-

1. ADS, New-York Historical Society.

In describing this document, Pendleton wrote: "The following paper, in the hand writing of Gen. Hamilton was inclosed with his will and some other papers in a packet addressed to one of his executors, which was of course not to have been delivered but in case of the melancholy event that has happened" (*New-York Evening Post,* July 16, 1804).

This document was the fourth item on the "List of Papers Given by Alexander Hamilton to Nathaniel Pendleton," July 19, 1804.

tinct from political opposition, which, as I trust, has proceeded from pure and upright motives.

Lastly, I shall hazard much, and can possibly gain nothing by the issue of the interview.

But it was, as I conceive, impossible for me to avoid it. There were *intrinsick* difficulties in the thing, and *artificial* embarrassments, from the manner of proceeding on the part of Col. Burr.

Intrinsick — because it is not to be denied, that my animadversions on the political principles character and views of Col Burr have been extremely severe, and on different occasions I, in common with many others, have made very unfavourable criticisms on particular instances of the private conduct of this Gentleman.

In proportion as these impressions were entertained with sincerity and uttered with motives and for purposes, which might appear to me commendable, would be the difficulty (until they could be removed by evidence of their being erroneous), of explanation or apology. The disavowal required of me by Col Burr, in a general and indefinite form, was out of my power, if it had really been proper for me to submit to be so questioned; but I was sincerely of opinion, that this could not be, and in this opinion, I was confirmed by that of a very moderate and judicious friend whom I consulted. Besides that Col Burr appeared to me to assume, in the first instance, a tone unnecessarily peremptory and menacing, and in the second positively offensive. Yet I wished, as far as might be practicable, to leave a door open to accommodation. This, I think, will be inferred from the written communications made by me and by my direction, and would be confirmed by the conversations between M^r van Ness and myself, which arose out of the subject.

I am not sure, whether under all the circumstances I did not go further in the attempt to accommodate, than a puntilious delicacy will justify. If so, I hope the motives I have stated will excuse me.

It is not my design, by what I have said to affix any odium on the conduct of Col Burr, in this case. He doubtless has heard of animadversions of mine which bore very hard upon him; and it is probable that as usual they were accompanied with some falshoods. He may have supposed himself under a necessity of acting as he has done. I hope the grounds of his proceeding have been such as ought to satisfy his own conscience.

I trust at the same time, that the world will do me the Justice to believe, that I have not answered him on light grounds, or from unworthy inducements. I certainly have had strong reasons for what I may have said, though it is possible that in some particulars, I may have been influenced by misconstruction or misinformation. It is also my ardent wish that I may have been more mistaken than I think I have been, and that he by his future conduct may shew himself worthy of all confidence and esteem, and prove an ornament and blessing to his Country.

As well because it is possible that I may have injured Col Burr, however convinced myself that my opinions and declarations have been well founded, as from my general principles and temper in relation to similar affairs — I have resolved, if our interview is conducted in the usual manner, and it pleases God to give me the opportunity, to *reserve* and *throw away* my first fire, and I *have thoughts* even of *reserving* my second fire — and thus giving a double opportunity to Col Burr to pause and to reflect.

It is not however my intention to enter into any explanations on the ground. Apology, from principle I hope, rather than Pride, is out of the question.

To those, who with me abhorring the practice of Duelling may think that I ought on no account to have added to the number of bad examples, I answer that my *relative* situation, as well in public as private appeals, inforcing all the considerations which constitute what men of the world denominate honor, impressed on me (as I thought) a peculiar necessity not to decline the call. The ability to be in future useful, whether in resisting mischief or effecting good, in those crises of our public affairs, which seem likely to happen, would probably be inseparable from a conformity with public prejudice in this particular.

A H

William P. Van Ness's Account of the Events of June 27–28, 1804[1]

I handed this[2] to him[3] at 12 O clock on Wednesday the 27th Instant. After he had perused it agreeable to my instructions I delivered the Message which it is unnecessary to repeat. The request it contained, was acceded to. After which Mr xxx remarked that a Court was then sitting in which Genl Hamilton had much business to transact, and had also some private arrangements to make which would render some delay unavoidable. I acceded to his wish, and Mr xxx said he would call on me again in the course of the day or the following morning to confer farther relative to time & place.

Thursday June 28th 10 clock P. M. Mr xxx called on me with a paper[4] he said contained some remarks on the letter I had yesterday delivered him. I replied that if the paper he offered contained a definite and specific proposition for an accomodation, I would with pleasure receive it and submit it to the consideration of my Principal. If not that I must decline taking it, Mr Burr viewed the correspondence completely terminated by the acceptance of the invitation contained in the Message I had yesterday delivered. Mr xxx replied that

1. "Van Ness's Narrative," AD, New York State Historical Association, Cooperstown, N.Y.

The contents of the "Draft of Van Ness's Narrative," although somewhat differently worded, are in all essentials the same as those of the "Narrative."

2. Van Ness to Pendleton, June 27, 1804.

3. Pendleton.

4. "Alexander Hamilton's Remarks on William P. Van Ness's Letter of June 27, 1804," June 28, 1804.

it did not contain any proposition of the kind I alluded to, but was a reply to my last letter. I of course declined receiving it. M^r xxx then took leave and said that he would call again in a day or two to arrange time and place.

Nathaniel Pendleton's Account of
the Events of June 27–28, 1804[1]

With this letter[2] a message was received, such as was to be expected, containing an invitation, which was accepted, and Mr. P. informed Mr. V. N. he should hear from him the next day as to further particulars.

This letter was delivered to Gen. H. on the same evening, and a very short conversation ensued between him and Mr. P. who was to call on him early the next morning for a further conference. When he did so, Gen. Hamilton said he had not understood whether the message and answer was definitely concluded, or whether another meeting was to take place for that purpose between Mr. P. and Mr. V. N. Under the latter impression, and as the last letter contained matter that naturally led to animadversion, he gave Mr. P. a paper[3] of remarks in his own hand writing, to be communicated to Mr. V. N. if the state of the affair rendered it proper.

In the farther interview with Mr. V. N. that day, after explaining the causes which had induced Gen. Hamilton to suppose that the state of the affair did not render it improper, he offered this paper to Mr. V. N.; but he declined receiving it, alledging, that he considered the correspondence as closed by the acceptance of the message that he had delivered.

1. *New-York Evening Post,* July 16, 1804.
2. Van Ness to Pendleton, June 27, 1804.
3. "Alexander Hamilton's Remarks on William P. Van Ness's Letter of June 27, 1804."

Mr. P. informed Mr. V. N. of the inducements mentioned by General Hamilton in those remarks, for the postponing of the meeting until the close of the Circuit; and as this was uncertain Mr. P. was to let him know when it would be convenient.

Alexander Hamilton's Remarks on William P. Van Ness's Letter of June 27, 1804[1]

[New York, June 28, 1804]

Remarks on the letter of June 27. 1804

Whether the observations in this letter are designed merely to justify the result, which is indicated in the close of the letter, or may be intended to give an opening for rendering any thing explicit which may have been deemed vague heretofore can only be judged of by the sequel. At any rate it appears to me necessary not to be misunderstood. M^r. Pendleton is therefore authorised to say that in the course of the present discussion, whether written or verbal, there has been no intention to evade defy or insult, but a sincere disposition to avoid extremities, if it could be done with propriety. With this view G H—— has been ready to enter into a frank and free explanation on any and every object of a specific nature; but not to answer a general and abstract inquiry, embracing a period too long for any accurate recollection, and exposing him to the unpleasant criticisms from or unpleasant discussions with any and every person, who may have understood him in an unfavourable sense. This (admitting that he could answer in a manner the most satisfactory to Col Burr) he should deem inadmissible, in principle and precedent, and humiliating in

1. AD, New-York Historical Society.

As noted in the preceding documents by both Van Ness and Pendleton, this document was offered by Pendleton to Van Ness on June 28, 1804, and Van Ness refused to accept it.

practice. To this therefore he can never submit. Frequent allusion has been made to slanders said to be in circulation. Whether they be openly or in whispers they have a form and shape and might be specified.

If the alternative alluded to in the close of the letter is definitively tendered, it must be accepted, the time place and manner to be afterwards regulated. I should not think it right in the midst of a circuit Court to withdraw my services from those who may have confided important interests to me and expose them to the embarrassment of seeking other counsel who may not have time to be sufficiently instructed in their causes. I shall also want a little time to make some arrangements respecting my own affairs.

William P. Van Ness's Account of the Events of July 3, 1804[1]

Tuesday July 3rd I again saw Mr Pendleton, and after a few subsequent interviews the time when the parties were to meet was ultimately fixed on for the morning of the 11th July Inst:

1. "Van Ness's Narrative," AD, New York State Historical Association, Cooperstown, N.Y.

In the draft of his "Narrative," Van Ness wrote:

Tuesday July 3, Mr Pendleton called and left his card upon seeing it at my office I imy waited on him he informed that the court would rise he supposed on Saturday the 7th Inst. and that on Monday or tuesday following Mr Hamilton would be ready to meet Mr Burr, and we agreed to ride out on thursday or friday to fix upon the ground. On Wednesday I wrote Mr Pend a Note of which No 15 [Van Ness to Pendleton, July 4, 1804] is a copy.

Alexander Hamilton to
Nathaniel Pendleton[1]

[New York, July 4, 1804]

I thank you My Dear Sir for your friendly offices in this last critical scene, if such it shall be. Excuse me for having inserted your name as Executor. I fear it may not be in your power to do much good to my family. But I am sure you will do all the good you can.

Y^{rs}. truly

A H

July 4. 1804

My most interesting papers in regard to my pecuniary affairs will be found

1 in the upper Apartment of Escrutory or Secretary in the Country
2 In a Box with pigeon holes in the room I occupy as an office.
3 In the Drawer of Press Bestead[2] in my house in Town.

1. ALS, New-York Historical Society.

This was item five in the "List of Papers Given by Alexander Hamilton to Nathaniel Pendleton," July 19, 1804.

2. I.e., a press bed.

Alexander Hamilton to
Elizabeth Hamilton[1]

[New York, July 4, 1804]

This letter, my very dear Eliza, will not be delivered to you, unless I shall first have terminated my earthly career; to begin, as I humbly hope from redeeming grace and divine mercy, a happy immortality.

If it had been possible for me to have avoided the interview, my love for you and my precious children would have been alone a decisive motive. But it was not possible, without sacrifices which would have rendered me unworthy of your esteem. I need not tell you of the pangs I feel, from the idea of quitting you and exposing you to the anguish which I know you would feel. Nor could I dwell on the topic lest it should unman me.

The consolations of Religion, my beloved, can alone support you; and these you have a right to enjoy. Fly to the bosom of your God and be comforted. With my last idea, I shall cherish the sweet hope of meeting you in a better world.

Adieu best of wives and best of Women. Embrace all my darling Children for me.

Ever yours
A H

July 4. 1804
Mrs. Hamilton

1. ALS, Hamilton Papers, Library of Congress.
This was part of item six in the "List of Papers Given by Alexander Hamilton to Nathaniel Pendleton," July 19, 1804.

William P. Van Ness to
Nathaniel Pendleton[1]

[New York, July 4, 1804]

Dr Sir

I have engaged two gentlemen to dine with me tomorrow. If it be perfectly immaterial to you, I should prefer taking our ride on some subsequent day.

I have the honor to be
Your Most ob^t & very
hon Sert.
W. P. Van Ness

Nath. Pendleton Esqr
July 4, 1804

1. ALS, New York State Historical Association, Cooperstown, N.Y.

Nathaniel Pendleton's Account of the Events of July 6, 9, 1804[1]

On Friday the 6th of July, the Circuit being closed, Mr. P. gave this information, and that Gen. Hamilton would be ready at any time after the Sunday following. On Monday the particulars were arranged, and the public are but too well acquainted with the sad result.

1. *New-York Evening Post,* July 16, 1804.

Aaron Burr to William P. Van Ness[1]

[New York, July 9, 1804]

I should with regret pass over another Day. It is
left however to your discretion. If the Fort is
agreed on, it will impossible to make an early
business without fatigue. What you shall do will be
satisfactory to me — except an early Morning hour.
I have no predilection for time. From 7 to 12 is the
least pleasant, but anything so we *but* get on.

If you go out, leave a time for me with your
servant saying when I shall see, or hear from, you

9 July

I don't see the necessity of *his* presence in order to
ultimate arrangements. He has confided this matter to P.

H——k[2] is enough, & soon that unnecessary.

1. AL, New York State Historical Association, Cooperstown, N.Y.
2. Dr. David Hosack, the physician who attended
Hamilton after he had been shot by Burr.

Last Will and Testament of
Alexander Hamilton[1]

[New York, July 9, 1804]

In the Name of God Amen! I Alexander Hamilton of the City of New York Counsellor at Law do make this my last Will and Testament as follows. First. I appoint John B Church Nicholas Fish and Nathaniel Pendleton of the City aforesaid Esquires to be Executors and Trustees of this my Will and I devise to them their heirs and Assigns, as joint Tenants and not as Tenants in common, All my Estate real and personal whatsoever and wheresoever upon Trust at their discretion to sell and dispose of the same, at such time and times in such manner and upon such terms as they the Survivors and Survivor shall think fit and out of the proceeds to pay all the Debts which I shall owe at the time of my decease, in whole, if the fund shall be sufficient, proportionally, if it shall be insufficient, and the residue, if any there shall be to pay and deliver to my excellent and dear Wife Elizabeth Hamilton.

Though if it shall please God to spare my life I may look for a considerable surplus out of my present property — Yet if he should speedily call me to the eternal Word, a forced sale as is usual may possibly render it insufficient to satisfy my Debts. I pray God that something may remain for

1. ADS, Hamilton Papers, Library of Congress.

This was the first item on the "List of Papers Given by Alexander Hamilton to Nathaniel Pendleton," July 19, 1804.

the maintenance and education of my dear Wife and Children. But should it on the contrary happen that there is not enough for the payment of my Debts, I entreat my Dear Children, if they or any of them shall ever be able to make up the Deficiency. I without hesitation commit to their delicacy a wish which is dictated by my own. Though conscious that I have too far sacrificed the interest of my family to public avocations & on this account have the less claim to burthen my Children, yet I trust in their magnanimity to appreciate as they ought this my request. In so unfavourable an event of things, the support of their dear Mother with the most respectful and tender attention is a duty all the sacredness of which they will feel. Probably her own patrimonial resources will preserve her from Indigence. But in all situations they are charged to bear in mind that she has been to them the most devoted and best of mothers — In Testimony whereof I have hereunto subscribed my hand the Ninth day of July in the year of our lord One thousand Eight hundred & four —

Signed sealed published & declared
as and for his last Will and Testa-
ment in our presence who have   Alexander
subscribed the same in his presence   Hamilton
 The words John B Church
 being above interlined —

Dominick F. Blake
Graham Newell
Theo B Valleau

Alexander Hamilton's Plan for
a Trust Fund[1]

[New York, July 9, 1804]

View of objects for which this trust is created & the value of the fund —

Objects

Bank accommodations to myself —	20,000	
To J Laurance — Ballance ℔ general Statemt. being 490 say 2/3 .	393	
Sum due to Marriage Contract of L L G[2]	269	
To *Sherrid* supposed[3]	1000	
To *Dash*[4]	512	
	22174	
Deduct on account of an additional provision made for J B Church to bring him to a level with other principal Indorser	1500	
		20674

Fund

Establist. at Haerlem which it is supposed would bring for Cash or moderate credit	25000	
deduct incumbrances . . .	12000	
		13000

---

1. AD, New-York Historical Society.

This was the second item on the "List of Papers Given by Alexander Hamilton to Nathaniel Pendleton," July 19, 1804.

2. Louis Le Guen.

3. Jacob Sherrid.

9000 acres in 15 & 21 probably
 bring 12 / ℔ acre in same manner   13500
other Articles (say)   3000
                                                    ─────
                                                    29.500

4. There is a John B. Dash, listed under the year 1803, in Hamilton's "Cash Book," Hamilton Papers, Library of Congress.

Letter of Hamilton to Burr, June 22, 1804.
Courtesy of The New-York Historical Society, New York City.

Assignment of Debts and Grant of Power of Attorney to John B. Church[1]

[New York, July 9, 1804]

Know all Men by these Presents, That I Alexander Hamilton of the City of New York Counsellor at law, in consideration of one Dollar to me in hand paid by John B Church Esquire, (the receipt whereof is hereby acknowledged) have bargained sold assigned and conveyed and hereby do bargain sell assign & convey to the said John B Church all and singular the debts due owing and payable to me which are specified in the schedule[2] hereunto annexed to be by him collected and the proceeds applied first towards the payment of all and every the debt and debts which I owe to my household and other servants and labourors and to the Woman who washes for Mrs. Hamilton and secondly towards the satisfaction and discharge of certain accommodation notes made by me and indorsed by him and which have been or shall be discounted in and by the Manhattan Bank and the Office of Discount & Deposit of the Bank of the United States in the City of New York. And for this purpose I do hereby constitute and appoint him my Attorney to ask demand sue for recover and receive the said debts or any part thereof to make and give acquittances. In witness whereof I have hereunto

1. ADS, Hamilton Papers, Library of Congress.

This was item seven on the "List of Papers Given by Alexander Hamilton to Nathaniel Pendleton," July 19, 1804.

2. See enclosure below.

subscribed & set my hand and seal the Ninth day of July in the year of our lord one thousand Eight hundred & four.

Sealed & delivered in presence of
Nathl. Pendleton

A Ham[ilton][3]

[Enclosure][4]

A Copy of a list of Debts assigned to John B Church Esquire per Deed Dated 9th July 1804 —

paid no	James & William Sterling	75
p^d	Isaac Clason	100
no	William Bell Robinson & Hartshorne	50
p^d	Mess. Jenkins (Riggs)	50
p^d	Pierre Van Cortland late L. Gouvenor ⎱	40
p^d.	P. Jay Monroe paid	40
p^d. no by TLO	Champlin & Smith (T L Ogden)	50
paid	Grullet ? & Bell credit 24–70	40
no	Out Door Underwriters including Hallet & Bowne adsm. Jenks (Pendleton) ⎱	200
	Assignees of Wm. L. Vandervort	250[5]

3. Manuscript mutilated. Letters in brackets have been inserted.

4. D, in unknown handwriting, Hamilton Papers, Library of Congress; also fragmentary DS in Hamilton's writing, Hamilton Papers, Library of Congress. The contents of the fragment are explained in notes 5 and 6 below.

5. The material beginning with this line and continu-

paid	400 by TLO	
	if Successful 250 more	
	Assignees of J Roget	50
	De Peyster ⎤	
paid	(Jones) ⎦	40
paid	Abijah Hammond ⎤	
	D A Ogden ⎦	40
p^d	Robert Cummings	75
paid	John McVickar	30
paid	Isaac Kibby	25
p^d	Hubbard ⎤	
	(Riggs) ⎦	50
p^d	Alexander Stewart	65
paid	Assignees of Kirkpatrick ⎤	
	(T. L. Ogden) by P. A. Carman ⎦	40
paid	George Stantan	30
paid L	Louis Simond	50
	John Hacker ⎤ 100 Pendleton paid	
	(Riker) ⎦	
paid	Ebenezer Stevens	50
paid	George Suckley	50
p^d	Bank of New York	100
p^d	James Arden	50
paid	William Thomas	25
paid	William Cooper	75
	William Byron p^d. 50	100
paid	Wm & Sylvester Robinson	250
p^d	Wm. Neilson	50
p^d.	John B. Graves	50

---

ing through the name William Byron has been taken from
the Hamilton fragment. The left-hand column of this portion, which designates those who paid, is not found on the
Hamilton fragment and has been taken from the copy.

paid no	James Shuter	50
by TLO	T L Ogden	
paid by no	Gouverneur including Insurance cause of Bauer? settled & compromised	100
paid	John Stewards note	51:46
		50^6
	D^s.	2490
	Henderson & Varick	20
	D^s.	2510

Particulars will better appear by
Account Book indorsed *M E M*

AH

July 9. 1804

6. The material beginning with this number through the end of the document has been taken from the Hamilton fragment. The left-hand column of this portion, which designates those who paid, is not found on the Hamilton fragment and has been taken from the copy.

Alexander Hamilton's Statement of His Pecuniary Affairs[1]

[New York, July 10, 1804]

Herewith is a general statement of my pecuniary affairs, in which there can be no material error. The result is that calculating my property at what it stands me in, I am now worth about Ten thousand pounds, and that estimating according to what my lands are now selling for and are likely to fetch, the surplus beyond my debts may fairly be stated at nearly double that sum. Yet I am pained to be obliged to entertain doubts, whether, if an accident should happen to me, by which the sales of my property should come, to be forced, it would be even sufficient to pay my debts.

In a situation like this, it is perhaps due to my reputation to explain why I have made so considerable an establishment in the country. This explanation shall be submitted.

1. ADS, RG 233, Records of the United States House of Representatives, National Archives.

This document was contained in a petition (for a claim based on Hamilton's military service) which Elizabeth Hamilton sent to Congress and which is dated January 10, 1816. Included in the petition is a statement by Pendleton that Hamilton's document was in a packet that also included Hamilton's will. Elizabeth Hamilton's petition and the Pendleton statement are both in the Records of the United States House of Representatives (RG 233), National Archives.

This was item three on the "List of Papers Given by Alexander Hamilton to Nathaniel Pendleton," July 19, 1804.

To men, who have been so much harassed in the busy world as myself, it is natural to look forward to a comfortable retirement, in the sequel of life, as a principal desideratum. This desire I have felt in the strongest manner; and to prepare for it has latterly been a favourite object. I thought that I might not only expect to accomplish the object, but might reasonably aim at it and pursue the preparatory measures, from the following considerations.

It has been for some time past pretty well ascertained to my mind, that the emoluments of my profession would prove equal to the maintenance of my family, and the gradual discharge of my debts, within a period to the end of which my faculties for business might be expected to extend, in full energy. I think myself warranted to estimate the annual product of those emoluments at Twelve [thousand] dollars at the least. My expences while the first improvements of my country establishment were going on have been great; but they would this summer and fall reach the point, at which it is my intention they should stop, at least 'till I should be better able than at present to add to them; and after a fair examination founded upon an actual account of my expenditures, I am persuaded that a plan I have contemplated for the next and succeeding years would bring my expences of every kind within the compass of four thousand Dollars yearly, exclusive of the interest of my country establishment. To this limit, I have been resolved to reduce them, even though it should be necessary to lease that establishment for a few years.

In the mean time, my lands now in a course of sale & settlement would accelerate the extinguishment of my debt, and in the end leave me a handsome clear property. It was also allowable for me to take into view, collaterally the expectations of my wife; which have been of late partly realised. She is now intitled to a property of between two and three thousand pounds (as I compute) by descent from her mother; and her father is understood to possess a large estate. I feel all the delicacy of this allusion; but the occasion I trust will plead my excuse. And that venerable father, I am sure, will pardon. He knows well all the nicety of my past conduct.

Viewing the matter in these different aspects, I trust the opinion of candid men will be, that there has been no impropriety in my conduct; especially when it is taken into the calculation that my Country establishment, though costly, promises, by the progressive rise of property on this Island, and the felicity of its situation, to become more and more valuable.

My chief apology is due to those friends, who have from mere kindness, indorsed my paper discounted at the Banks. On mature reflection I have thought it jusfiable to secure them in preference to other Creditors, lest perchance there should be *a deficit*. Yet while this may save them from eventual loss, it will not exempt them from some present inconvenience. As to this I can only throw myself upon their kindness and entreat the indulgence of the Banks for them. Perhaps this request may be supposed intitled to some regard.

In the event, which would bring this paper to

the public eye, one thing at least would be put beyond a doubt. This is, that my public labours have amounted to an absolute sacrifice of the interests of my family, and that in all pecuniary concerns the delicacy, no less than the probity of my conduct in public stations, has been such as to defy even the shadows of a question.

Indeed, I have not enjoyed the ordinary advantages incident to my military services. Being a member of Congress, while the question of the commutation of the half pay of the army for a sum in gross was in debate, delicacy and a desire to be useful to the army, by removing the idea of my having an interest in the question, induced me to write to the Secretary of War and relinquish my claim to half pay; which, or the equivalent, I have accordingly never received. Neither have I ever applied for the lands allowed by the United States to Officers of my rank. Nor did I ever obtain from this state the allowance of lands made to officers of similar rank. It is true that having served through the latter period of the War on the general staff of the UStates and not in the line of this State, I could not claim that allowance as a matter of course. But have before the War resided in this State and having entered the military career at the head of a company of Artillery raised for the particular defence of this State, I had better pretensions to the allowance than others to whom it was actually made. Yet has it not been extended to me.

A H.

Alexander Hamilton's Statement of His Property and Debts[1]

[New York, July 10, 1804]

Statement of my property and Debts July 1. 1804 —

Real Estate

My share of Townships Nᵒ. 9. 10. 15. 17 and 21 in Scribas Patent in connection with J B Church and John Laurance viz 1/6 of the first purchase the whole being 31528 acres & ¼ of an acre & one third of the residuary purchase upon the suit in chancery being together nearly 20000 acres which now stand me in about } 33000 —

My ¼ of purchase in Nobleborough together with J Laurance Robert Troupe & N Fish being 5450 accres computed now to stand me in abᵗ. } 9000 —

Five shares of lands in the Ohio Company being about 6000 acres purchased chiefly with a certificate for my own services & estimated to now stand me in . . . . } 6000 —

4 lots in the city of New York being the moiety of 8 lots purchased of J Riley the other moiety for J B Church now stand me in about 1800
deduct a subsisting morgage thereupon not precisely recollected suppose . 650   1150

1. ADS, New-York Historical Society.
This was part of the third item on the "List of Papers Given by Alexander Hamilton to Nathaniel Pendleton," July 19, 1804.

My establishment in the Country *at
Harlem* estimated to now stand me in
about . . . . } 25000

Dollars   74150

Personal Estate

Furniture and Library . . . . .   3000 —
Horses and Carriages . . . .   600 —

Good Debts

Due me from W Greene on account of a
Purchase of Trustee of Ringwood Company on the Guaranty of P. Schuyler &
others & as principal & interest ab^t 500
deduct this sum still unpaid
to Trustees ab 250   250

D^s 3850

Estimated cost of real Estate   D^s 74150
Personal Estate 3850
Due me for professional services
say 2500   6350

Dollars   80500

Debts which I owe

1. To the several Banks in the city of
   New York   20000
2. To Gilchrist & Fowler (suppose) . .   10000
3. To Richard Harrison and Aaron
   Ogden as Trustees for Louis Le
   Guen & his wife secured by Mortgage } 5350
   on my house
   5000 D^s. with one years interest . .
4. To the same for this sum passed to
   my Credit on a Bank of U States on } 269.57
   account of 6 ⅌ C^t. stock
5. To Louis Le Guen, the sum borrowed of him ⅌ my Note (a years in- } 3000. —
   terest being paid)

6	To Herman Le Roy Mortgage to Schiefflen assigned to him . . 4000		
	years interest nearly due . . . 280		4280 —
7	To J B Church per account June 23.		
	1803 . . . . 3000.60		
	Interest for a year 210		
		3210.60	
	Due me per my Book suppose . 600 —		
	(page 63)		2610
8	To Nicholas Fish suppose		1500 —
9	To Victor Du Pont per my bond ab^t		1000 —
	My Note to him payable 1 Aug		800
			48809.57
10	To S Bradhust for part of my County seat purchased of him principal & half a years interest (say)		3110 —
11	To Jacob Sherrid probably . . .		1000
12	To John Laurance for two thirds of an accommodation Note discounted at the Merc^ts. Bank (say) . . 600 —		
	Deduct what he owes me ⅌ acc^t 110		490
13	To J B Dash Junr. ⅌ Note		512.32
	Miscellany		800
			5472²²
	Ballance in my favour Dollars		2577⁷⁸

Remarks

N⁰. 2. The sum due to Fowler & Gilchrist is on account of a purchase under a mortgage which they had upon a tract of land including that which was bought by Church Laurance & myself. By agreement this money was payable by installments. For the first I gave them my notes which have been paid, though they retain the bond for that installment, which ought to be delivered up. The remaining installments are to be paid — the first one is now due.

N⁰. 7 Sometime last fall, I authorised J B Church to sell my four lots if they would bring each 200 pounds & apply the proceeds to my credit. Since that I have verbally told him that he might sell them at whatever he should be willing to sell his own for. I consider what has been done as amounting to an appropriation of these lots toward the payment of his Debt and so has been my intention. I have hesitated indeed whether I ought not now to do a definitive act to effect this object. But on reflection I thought it adviseable to leave things in *status quo* with this explanation.

As to Item N⁰. 4 of my debts, I have thought it right to put it on the same foot with my bank accommodations because it is part of a Trust fund being the 2 per Cent which was paid on account of the *principal* of the Stock, for which reason it was not paid over to M^r Le Guen. But I think I have made a mistake in paying the full interest as received since from the Constitution of the public debt a part of this must represent the remaining principal. If there be any error M^r. Le Guen will readily replace it or it can be retained out of the sum I owe him individually. I have been rather negligent as to the entry of my remittances but except payments amounting to a few dollars he has had as I believe all I have received for him on account of the trust fund or otherwise not noted in this paper. This he will himself put right & indeed may be collected from his letters.

I have thought it right to do the like as to Item N⁰ 12 because in fact this is a joint accommodation

note. So also as to 11 & 13 because the labour &
supplies of these parties have contributed to form
that fund being for the purpose of my house &c at
Haerlem.

Alexander Hamilton to
Elizabeth Hamilton[1]

[New York, July 10, 1804]

My beloved Eliza

M*rs*. Mitchel[2] is the person in the world to whom as a friend I am under the greatest Obligations. I have [*not*][3] hitherto done my [*duty*] to her. But [*resolved to*] repair my omission as much as [*possible*] I have encouraged her to come to [*this country*] and intend, if it shall be [*in my power*] to render the Evening of her days comfortable. But if it shall please God to put this out of my power and to inable you hereafter to be of service to her, I entreat you to do it and to treat her with the tenderness of a Sister.

1. ALS, Hamilton Papers, Library of Congress.

This was part of item six on the "List of Papers Given by Alexander Hamilton to Nathaniel Pendleton," July 19, 1804.

2. Ann Mitchell, Hamilton's cousin, was the daughter of James Lytton, of St. Croix. Lytton died in 1769. In 1763 Ann Mitchell left St. Croix for New York with her first husband, John Venton. In 1770 she returned to St. Croix to claim her share of her father's estate. It was at this time that she first became acquainted with Hamilton. Venton died in 1777, and three years later she married George Mitchell, a native of Scotland, who had migrated from Virginia to St. Croix. Once again she came to the United States — probably in 1783 — and settled in Burlington, New Jersey.

For July 11, 1796, there is the following entry in Hamilton's "Cash Book" (Hamilton Papers, Library of Congress): "Donation to my Cozen Mrs Mitchell; draft upon me $100."

3. All italicized bracketed material in this letter taken from a transcript of it in JCH Transcripts.

This is my second letter.

The Scruples [*of a Christian have deter*]mined me to expose my own [*life to any*] extent rather than subject my[*self to the*] guilt of taking the life of [*another*]. This must increase my hazards & redoubles my pangs for you. But you had rather I should die innocent than live guilty. Heaven can [*preserve*] me [*and I humbly*] hope will, but in the contrary event, I charge you to remember that you are a Christian. God's will be done! The will of a merciful God must be good.

Once more Adieu My Darling
darling Wife
AH
Tuesday Evening 10 O Cl[*ock*]

[*Mrs Ha*]milton

Aaron Burr to Theodosia Burr Alston[1]

New-York, July 10, 1804

Having lately written my will, and given my private letters and papers in charge to you, I have no other direction to give you on the subject but to request you to burn all such as, if by accident made public, would injure any person. This is more particularly applicable to the letters of my female correspondents. All my letters, and copies of letters, of which I have retained copies, are in six blue boxes. If your husband[2] or any one else (no one, however, could do it so well as he) should think it worth while to write a sketch of my life, some materials will be found among these letters.

Tell my dear Natalie[3] that I have not left her anything, for the very good reason that I had nothing to leave to any one. My estate will just about pay my debts and no more — I mean, if I should die this year. If I live a few years, it is probable things may be better. Give Natalie one of the pictures of me. There are three in this house; that of Stewart, and two by Vanderlyn. Give her any other little tokens she may desire. One of those pictures, also, I pray you to give to Doctor Eustis.[4] To Bartow[5] something — what you please.

1. Matthew L. Davis (ed.), *Memoirs of Aaron Burr* (New York, 1855), II, 322–324.

2. Joseph Alston. On this day Burr also wrote Alston, who had been appointed one of the executors of Burr's estate (*ibid.*, 324–326).

3. Natalie De Lage Sumter, a French refugee who was adopted by Burr. She married Thomas Sumter, Jr., the son of General Thomas Sumter of South Carolina.

I pray you and your husband to convey to Peggy[6] the small lot, not numbered, which is the fourth article mentioned in my list of property. It is worth about two hundred and fifty dollars. Give her also fifty dollars in cash as a reward for her fidelity. Dispose of Nancy[6] as you please. She is honest, robust, and good-tempered. Peter[6] is the most intelligent and best-disposed black I have ever known. (I mean the black boy I bought last fall from Mr. Turnbull.) I advise you, by all means, to keep him as the valet of your son. Persuade Peggy to live with you if you can.

I have desired that my wearing apparel be given to Frederic.[7] Give him also a sword or pair of pistols.

Burn immediately a small bundle, tied with a red string, which you will find in the little flat writing-case — that which we used with the curricle. The bundle is marked *"Put."*

The letters of *Clara*[8] (the greatest part of them) are tied up in a white handkerchief, which you will find in the blue box No. 5. You may hand them to Mari, if you please. My letters to Clara are in the same bundle. You, and by-and-by Aaron Burr Alston,[9] may laugh at *gamp* when you look over this nonsense.

4. Probably Dr. William Eustis.

5. John Bartow Prevost, Burr's stepson.

6. Peggy, Nancy, and Peter were Burr's slaves.

7. Augustine James Frederick Prevost, Burr's stepson.

8. The various and numerous women in Burr's life are unidentifiable because of the destruction, at Burr's request, of all personal correspondence by Matthew L. Davis.

9. Burr's grandson.

Many of the letters of *Clara* will be found among my ordinary letters, filed and marked, sometimes *"Clara,"* sometimes "L."

I am indebted to you, my dearest Theodosia, for a very great portion of the happiness which I have enjoyed in this life. You have completely satisfied all that my heart and affections had hoped or even wished. With a little more perseverence, determination, and industry, you will obtain all that my ambition or vanity had fondly imagined. Let your son have occasion to be proud that he had a mother. Adieu. Adieu.

A. Burr

I have directed that the flat writing-case and the blue box No. 5, both in the library, be opened only by you. There are six of these blue boxes which contain my letters and copies of letters, except those two clumsey quarto volumes, in which letter-press copies are pasted. They are somewhere in the library. The keys of the other five boxes are in No. 5.

It just now occurs to me to give poor dear Frederic my watch. I have already directed my executors here to give him my wearing apparel. When you come hither you must send for Frederic, and open your whole heart to him. He loves *me* almost as much as Theodosia does; and he does love *you* to adoration.

I have just now found four packets of letters between *Clara and Mentor* besides those in the handkerchief. I have thrown them loose into box No. 5. What a medley you will find in that box!

The seal of the late George Washington, which you will find in the blue box No. 5, was given to me by Mr. and Mrs. Law.[10] You may keep it for your son, or give it to whom you please.

Assure Mrs. Law of my latest recollection. Adieu. Adieu.

A. Burr.

10. Mr. and Mrs. Thomas Law of Washington, D.C.

Memorandum of Fees Received by Alexander Hamilton since His Engagement[1]

[New York, July 10, 1804]

These sums having been received since my *engagement* & no services rendered I confide them as forming part of my debts

Franklin & Robinson	50 —
James Amory	20 —
D Ludlow & Cº	50 —
Wilmerding	30 —
Murdoch Masterston & Cº	20 —
Steven Ray & David Dill	25 —
Scott & Tremaine	20 —

A Hamilton
July 10, 1804

1. ADS, New-York Historical Society.

This was the tenth item on the "List of Papers Given by Alexander Hamilton to Nathaniel Pendleton," July 19, 1804.

Nathaniel Pendleton's Statement of the Regulations for the Duel Between Alexander Hamilton and Aaron Burr[1]

[New York, July 10, 1804][2]

1. The parties will leave town tomorrow morning about five oClock, and meet at the place agreed on. The party arriving first shall wait for the other.

2. The weapons shall be pistols not exceeding Eleven inches in the barrel. The distance ten paces.

3. The Choice of positions to be determined by lot.

4. The parties having taken their positions one of the seconds to be determined by lot (after having ascertained that both parties are ready) shall loudly and distinctly give the word "present" — If one of the parties fires, and the other hath not fired, the opposite second shall say one, two, three, fire, and he shall then fire or lose his shot. A snap or flash is a fire.

Monday.

11 July 1804

1. AD, New-York Historical Society.

2. Although Pendleton dated this document July 11 at the bottom of the page, the first sentence indicates that it was written on the preceding day.

Statement for Press Prepared Immediately after the Duel by Nathaniel Pendleton and William P. Van Ness[1]

[New York, July 11, 1804]

Col: Burr arrived first on the ground as had been previously agreed. When Gen¹ Hamilton arrived the parties exchanged salutations and the Seconds proceeded to make their arrangements. They measured the distance, ten full paces, and cast lots for the choice of position as also to determine by whom the word should be given, both of which fell to the Second of Gen¹ Hamilton. They then proceeded to load the pistols in each others presence, after which the parties took their stations. The Gentleman who was to give the word, then

1. AD, in the writing of Van Ness, New York State Historical Association, Cooperstown, N.Y.; also AD, in the writing of Pendleton, New-York Historical Society.

This document was printed in the New York *Morning Chronicle,* July 17, 1804; and in the *New-York Evening Post,* July 19, 1804.

The Pendleton version, which is incomplete, reads as follows:

Col° Burr arrived first on the ground as had been previously agreed. When General Hamilton arrived the parties exchanged salutations, and the Seconds proceeded to make their arrangements.

They measured the distance ten full paces, and cast lots for the choice of position, as also to determine by whom the word should be given, both of which fell to the second of General Hamilton. They then proceeded to load the Pistols in each others presence after which the parties took their Stations. The Gentleman who was to give the word then explained to the par-

explained to the parties the rules which were to govern them in firing which were as follows:

The parties being placed at their stations — The Second who gives the word shall ask them whether they are ready — being answered in the affirmative, he shall say *"present"* after which the parties shall present & fire when they please. If one fires before the opposite second shall say one two, three, fire, and he shall fire or loose his fire.

And asked if they were prepared, being answered in the affirmative he gave the word *present* as had been agreed on, and both of the parties took aim & fired in succession. The intervening time is not expressed as the seconds do not precisely agree on that point. The pistols were discharged within a few seconds of each other and the fire of Col: Burr took effect; Genl Hamilton almost instantly fell,[2] Col: Burr then advanced toward Genl H——n

---

ties the rules which were to govern them in firing, which were as follows. "The parties being placed at their Stations, the second who gives the word shall ask them if they are ready — being answered in the Affirmative he shall say 'present' after which the parties shall present & fire when they please. If one fires before the other the opposite second shall say, one, two, three, fire, and he shall fire or lose his fire." The Gentleman who was to give the word asked if they were prepared, being answered in the Affirmative he gave the word "present." Both the parties presented. The Pistols were both discharged successively, (but the time intervening between the two is not here Stated the seconds not agreeing in that fact). The fire of Col°.

2. Parts of this sentence, as originally written, were crossed out. The sentence, as originally written, read

with a manner and gesture that appeared to Gen[l] Hamilton's friend to be expressive of regret, but without Speaking turned about & withdrew — Being urged from the field by his friend as has been subsequently stated, with a view to prevent his being recognised by the Surgeon and Bargemen who were then approaching.[3] No farther communication took place between the principals and the Barge that carried Col: Burr immediately returned to the City. We conceive it proper to add that the conduct of the parties in that interview was perfectly proper as suited the occasion.[4]

". . . [and] the body of Genl Hamilton who instantly fell . . . ." "Almost," which is substituted for "who," is in the writing of Pendleton.

3. Parts of this sentence as originally written were crossed out, and insertions were added. The sentence, as originally written, read ". . . Col: Burr then advanced toward gentleman with an expression of concern on his countenance and gestures, but was stopped by his Second with a view as has been subsequently stated to prevent his being recognized by the Surgeon and Bargemen who were then approaching." The insertions are partially in the writing of Pendleton.

4. Parts of this sentence, as originally written, were crossed out, and insertions were added. The sentence, as originally written, read: ". . . the conduct of both parties was perfectly correct and honorable." The insertions are in the writing of Pendleton.

Aaron Burr to Dr. David Hosack[1]

[New York, July 12, 1804]

M^r. Burr's respectful Compliments. He requests D^r. Hosack to inform him of the present state of Genl. H. and of the hopes which are entertained of his recovery.

M^r. Burr begs to know at what hours of the [day] the D^r. may most probably be found at home, that he may repeat his inquiries. He would take it very kind if the D^r. would take the trouble of calling on him as he returns from M^r. Bayard's.[2]

Thursday

12 July

1. AL, Mr. John Hampton Barnes, Philadelphia.

2. William Bayard, a New York merchant, who was a member of the firm of LeRoy, Bayard & McEvers, for which Hamilton had frequently served as an attorney. Hamilton was taken to Bayard's house at 80–82 Jane Street immediately after the duel. It was here that Hamilton died.

Benjamin Moore to William Coleman[1]

[New York] Thursday evening, July 12.

Mr. Coleman,

The public mind being extremely agitated by the melancholy fate of that great man, ALEXANDER HAMILTON, I have thought it would be grateful to my fellow-citizens, would provide against misrepresentation, and, perhaps, be conducive to the advancement of the cause of Religion, were I to give a narrative of some facts which have fallen under my own observation, during the time which elapsed between the fatal duel and his departure out of this world.

Yesterday morning, immediately after he was brought from Hoboken to the house of Mr. Bayard,[2] at Greenwich, a message was sent informing me of the sad event, accompanied by a request from General Hamilton, that I would come to him for the purpose of administering the holy communion. I went; but being desirous to afford time for serious reflection, and conceiving that under existing circumstances, it would be right and proper to avoid every appearance of precipitancy in performing one of the most solemn offices of our religion, I did not then comply with his desire. At one o'clock I was again called on to visit him.

1. *New-York Evening Post,* July 13, 1804.
Benjamin Moore was the second Protestant Episcopal bishop of New York and the president of Columbia College. William Coleman, editor of the *New-York Evening Post,* was a close friend of Hamilton.
2. William Bayard.

Upon my entering the room and approaching his bed, with the utmost calmness and composure he said, "My dear Sir, you perceive my unfortunate situation, and no doubt have been made acquainted with the circumstances which led to it. It is my desire to receive the Communion at your hands. I hope you will not conceive there is any impropriety in my request." He added, "It has for some time past been the wish of my heart, and it was my intention to take an early opportunity of uniting myself to the church, by the reception of that holy ordinance." I observed to him, that he must be very sensible of the delicate and trying situation in which I was then placed; that however desirous I might be to afford consolation to a fellow mortal in distress; still, it was my duty as a minister of the gospel, to hold up the law of God as paramount to all other law; and that, therefore, under the influence of such sentiments, I must unequivocally condemn the practice which had brought him to his present unhappy condition. He acknowledged the propriety of these sentiments, and declared that he viewed the late transaction with sorrow and contrition. I then asked him, "Should it please God, to restore you to health, Sir, will you never be again engaged in a similar transaction? and will you employ all your influence in society to discountenance this barbarous custom?" His answer was, "That, Sir, is my deliberate intention."

I proceeded to converse with him on the subject of his receiving the Communion; and told him that with respect to the qualifications of those who wished to become partakers of that holy ordinance, my enquiries could not be made in language more expressive than that which was used by our Church. "Do you sincerely repent of your sins past? Have you a lively faith in God's mercy through Christ, with a thankful remembrance of the death of Christ? And are you disposed to live in love and charity with all men?" He lifted up his hands and said, "With the utmost sincerity of heart I can answer those questions in the affirmative — I have no ill will against Col. Burr. I met him with a fixed resolution to do him no harm — I forgive all that happened." I then observed to him, that the terrors of the divine law were to be announced to the obdurate and impenitent: but that the consolations of the Gospel were to be offered to the humble and contrite heart: that I had no reason to doubt his sincerity, and would proceed immediately to gratify his wishes. The Communion was then administered, which he received with great devotion, and his heart afterwards appeared to be perfectly at rest. I saw him again this morning, when, with his last faultering words, he expressed a strong confidence in the mercy of God through the intercession of the Redeemer. I remained with him until 2 o'clock this afternoon, when death closed the awful scene — he expired without a struggle, and almost without a groan.

By reflecting on this melancholy event, let the humble believer be encouraged ever to hold fast that precious faith which is the only source of true consolation in the last extremity of nature. Let the Infidel be persuaded to abandon his opposition to that gospel which the strong, inquisitive, and comprehensive mind of a HAMILTON embraced, in his last moments, as the truth from heaven. Let those who are disposed to justify the practice of duelling, be induced, by this simple narrative, to view with abhorrence that custom which has occasioned an irreparable loss to a worthy and most afflicted family; which has deprived his friends of a beloved companion, his profession of one of its brightest ornaments, and his country of a great statesman and a real patriot.

With great respect,
I remain your friend and servant,
BENJAMIN MOORE

List of Papers Given by Alexander Hamilton to Nathaniel Pendleton[1]

[New York, July 19, 1804]

There were inclosed under this cover and delivered to me after the death of General Hamilton

1. His will —[2]
2. Deed of trust to John B Church, Jn⁰ Laurence, & Gen¹ Clarkson[3]
3. State of his Property & Debts with remarks[4]
4. Remarks explanatory of his conduct Motives & views in his expected interview[5]
5. Note to Myself[6]
6. Letter to Mrs. Hamilton[7]
7. Letter to John B. Church inclosing an assignment of some debts.[8]
8. Letter to Mrs. Mitchell inclosing 400 dollars as was mentioned on the outside. Sealed[9]
9. Letter to Geo. Mitchell inclosing a lottery ticket. as mentioned on the outside. Sealed.[10]

1. ADS, New-York Historical Society.

2. See "Last Will and Testament of Alexander Hamilton," July 9, 1804.

3. See "Alexander Hamilton's Plan for a Trust Fund," July 9, 1804. This is probably only a fragment of the "Deed of Trust to John B. Church, Jn⁰ Laurence, & Gen¹ Clarkson" referred to on this list.

4. See "Alexander Hamilton's Statement of His Pecuniary Affairs," July 10, 1804, and "Alexander Hamilton's Statement of his Property and Debts," July 10, 1804.

5. See "Alexander Hamilton's Remarks on his Impending Duel with Aaron Burr," June 27–July 4, 1804.

6. See Hamilton to Pendleton, July 4, 1804.

7. Hamilton wrote two letters to Elizabeth Hamilton which were to be delivered after his death. This packet

10. Memorandum of some fees received after his Engagement which he considers as part of his debts —[11]

> The packet was opened by me in the presence of David A. Ogden and Washington Morton on the day of his death —
>
> Nath[l]. Pendleton
> Made July 19th. 1804

---

probably contained them both. See Hamilton to Elizabeth Hamilton, July 4, 1804, and July 10, 1804.

8. See "Assignment of Debts and Grant of Power of Attorney to John B. Church," July 9, 1804. The enclosing letter is missing.

9. Letter missing.

10. Letter missing.

11. See "Memorandum of Fees Received by Alexander Hamilton since His Engagement," July 10, 1804.

Nathaniel Pendleton's Amended Version of His and William P. Van Ness's Statement of July 11, 1804[1]

[New York, July 19, 1804]

The statement containing the facts that led to the interview between General Hamilton and Col. Burr, published in the Evening Post on Monday, studiously avoided mentioning any particulars of what past at the place of meeting. This was dictated by suitable considerations at the time, and with the intention, that whatever it might be deemed proper to lay before the public, should be made the subject of a future communication. The following is therefore now submitted.

In the interviews that have since taken place between the gentlemen that were present, they have not been able to agree in two important facts that passed there — for which reason nothing was said on those subjects in the paper lately published as to other particulars in which they were agreed.

Mr. P. expressed a confident opinion that General Hamilton did not fire first — and that he did not fire at all *at Col. Burr*. Mr. V. N. seemed equally confident in the opinion that Gen. H. did fire first — and of course that it must have been *at* his antagonist.

General Hamilton's friend thinks it to be a sacred duty he owes to the memory of that exalted man, to his country, and his friends, to publish to the world such facts and circumstances as have pro-

1. *New-York Evening Post,* July 19, 1804.

duced a decisive conviction in his own mind, that he cannot have been mistaken in the belief he has formed on these points —

1st. Besides the testimonies of Bishop Moore, and the paper containing an express declaration, under General Hamilton's own hand, enclosed to his friend in a packet, not to be delivered but in the event of his death, and which have already been published, General Hamilton informed Mr. P. at least ten days previous to the affair, that he had doubts whether he would not receive and not return Mr. Burr's first fire. Mr. P. remonstrated against this determination, and urged many considerations against it, as dangerous to himself and not necessary in the particular case, when every ground of accomodation, not humiliating, had been proposed and rejected. He said he would not decide lightly, but take time to deliberate fully. It was incidentally mentioned again at their occasional subsequent conversations, and on the evening preceding the time of the appointed interview, he informed Mr. P. he had made up his mind *not to fire at Col. Burr the first time, but to receive his fire, and fire in the air.* Mr. P. again urged him upon this subject, and repeated his former arguments. His final answer was in terms that made an impression on Mr. P's mind which can never be effaced. "My friend, it is the effect of a RELIGIOUS SCRUPLE, and does not admit of reasoning, it is useless to say more on the subject, as my purpose is definitely fixed."

2d. His last words before he was wounded afford a proof that this purpose had not changed. When he received his pistol, after having taken his position, he was asked if he would have the hair spring set? — His answer was, *"Not this time."*

3d. After he was wounded, and laid in the boat, the first words he uttered after recovering the power of speech, were, (addressing himself to a gentleman present, who perfectly well remembers it) *"Pendleton knows I did not mean to fire at Col. Burr the first time."*

4th. This determination had been communicated by Mr. P. to that gentleman that morning, before they left the city.

5th. The pistol that had been used by General Hamilton, lying loose over the other apparatus in the case which was open; after having been some time in the boat, one of the boatmen took hold of it to put it into the case. General Hamilton observing this, said *"Take care of that pistol — it is cocked. It may go off and do mischief."* This is also remembered by the Gentleman alluded to.

This shews that he was not sensible of having fired at all. If he had fired *previous* to receiving the wound, he would have remembered it, and therefore have known that the pistol could not go off; but if *afterwards* it must have been the effect of an involuntary exertion of the muscles produced by a mortal wound, in which case, he could not have been conscious of having fired.

6. Mr. P having so strong a conviction that if General Hamilton had fired first, it could not have escaped his attention (all his anxiety being alive for the effect of the first fire, and having no reason to believe the friend of Col. Burr was not sincere in the contrary opinion) he determined to go to the spot where the affair took place, to see if he could

not discover some traces of the course of the ball from Gen. Hamilton's pistol. He took a friend with him the day after General Hamilton died, and after some examination they fortunately found what they were in search of. They ascertained that the ball passed through the limb of a cedar tree, at an elevation of about twelve feet and a half, perpendicularly from the ground, between thirteen and fourteen feet from the mark on which General Hamilton stood, and about four feet wide of the direct line between him and Col. Burr, on the right side; he having fallen on the left. The part of the limb through which the ball passed was cut off and brought to this city, and is now in Mr. Church's possession.

No inferences are pointed out as resulting from these facts, nor will any comments be made. They are left to the candid judgment and feelings of the public.

William P. Van Ness's Amended Version of His and Nathaniel Pendleton's Statement of July 11, 1804[1]

The second of G H having considered it proper to subjoin an explanatory note to the statement mutually furnished, it becomes proper for the gentleman who attended Col Burr to state also his impressions with respect to those points on which their exists a variance of opinion. In doing this he pointedly disclaims any idea disrespectful to the memory of G H, or an intention to ascribe any conduct to him that is not in his opinion perfectly honorable & correct.

The parties met as has been above related & took their respective stations as directed: the pistols were then handed to them by the seconds. Gen Hamilton elevated his, as if to try the light,[2] & lowering it said I beg pardon for delaying you but the direction of the line renders it necessary, at the same time feeling his pockets with his left hand, & drawing forth his spectacles put them on. The second then asked if they were prepared which was replied to in the affirmative. The word *present* was then given, on which both parties took aim, the pistol of General Hamilton was first discharged and Col Burr fired immediately after, only five or six seconds of time intervening. On this point the second of Col Burr has full & perfect recollection, he noticed particularly the discharge of

1. AD, New York State Historical Society, Cooperstown, N.Y.

2. In the manuscript the word "position" is written over the word "light," apparently an alternate choice.

G H's pistol, & looked to his principal to ascertain whether he was hurt, he then clearly saw Col B s pistol discharged. At the moment of looking at Col B on the discharge of G H's pistol he perceived a slight motion in his person, which induced the idea of his being struck, on this point he conversed with his principal on their return, who ascribed that circumstance to a small stone under his foot, & observed that the smoke of G Hs pistol obscured him for a moment previous to his firing.

When G H fell Col B advanced toward him as stated & was checked by his second who urged the importance of his immediately repairing to the barge, conceiving that G H was mortally wounded, & being desirous to secure his principal from the sight of the surgeon & bargemen who might be called in evidence. Col B complied with his request.

He shortly followed him to the boat, and Col B again expressed a wish to return, saying with an expression of much concern, I must go & speak to him. I again urged the obvious impropriety stating that the G was surrounded by the Surgeon & Bargemen by whom he must not be seen & insisted on immediate departure.

Coroner's Inquest on the Death of Alexander Hamilton[1]

[New York, August 2, 1804]

City & County of New York } ss

An Inquisition Indented taken for the People of the State of New york

At the third Ward of the City of New york in the County of New york, the thirteenth day of July in the Year of Our Lord One thousand Eight hundred and four, and Continued by adjournment until the Second day of August in the Year Aforesaid, before me John Burger Coroner for the Said City and County of New york, On View of the body of Alexander Hamilton, then and there to wit on the Said thirteenth day of July in the year last aforesaid, at the Ward City and County aforesaid lying dead, Upon the Oath of Alexander Anderson, George Minuse, John A Hardenbrook, Peter Bonnett, Elam Williams, John Coffin, John Mildeberger, David A Brower, David Lydig, Abraham Bloodgood, James Cummings, Amos Curtis, Isaac Burr Benjamin Strong and John D. Miller.

Good and Lawful men of the said City and County of New York, duly chosen and Who being then and there duly sworn and Charged to enquire for the People of the State of New york, When Where how and by What means the said, Alexander Hamilton, Came to his death, do Upon their

1. DS, in unknown handwriting, Mr. C. P. G. Fuller, New York City. Mr. Fuller recently gave this document to Princeton University.

Oath say that Aaron Burr, late of the Eighth Ward of the said City in the said County Esquire and Vice President of the United States, not having the fear of God before his eyes, but being moved and seduced by the Instigation of the devil, on the eleventh day of July in the year last aforesaid, with force and Arms, in the County of Bergen and State of New Jersey in and upon the Said Alexander Hamilton in the peace of God and of the people, of the Said State of New Jersey, then and there being, feloniously Wilfully and of his Malice aforethought, did make an Assault, and that the Said Aaron Burr, a Certain Pistol of the Value of One Dollar Charged and loaded With Gun powder and a leaden bullet which he the Said Aaron Burr, then and there had and held in his right hand, to, at, and against the right-side of the Belly of the Said Alexander Hamilton did then and there shoot off and discharge, by means Whereof he the Said Aaron Burr feloniously Wilfully and of his Malice Aforethought, did then and there give Unto him the Said Alexander Hamilton, With the leaden bullet aforesaid so as aforesaid Shot off and discharged out of the Pistol aforesaid by the force of the Gun powder aforesaid upon the right side of the belly of him the said Alexander Hamilton a little above the Hip, one Mortal Wound, penetrating the Belly of him the Said Alexander Hamilton of Which said Mortal wound he the said Alexander Hamilton, from the said Eleventh day of July in the year aforesaid, until the twelfth day of July, in the same Year, as Well in the County of Bergen in the State of New Jersey, aforesaid, as also at the Eighth Ward of the City of New york in the County of New york aforesaid did languish and languishing did live; on Which twelfth day of July in the said year the Said Alexander Hamilton at the Said Eighth Ward of the said City in the Said County of New york, of the Mortal Wound aforesaid died, and the Jurors aforesaid on their Oath aforesaid do further say that William P Van Ness late of the first Ward of the City of New york in the County of New york aforesaid Attorney at Law, and Nathaniel Pendleton late of the Same place Counsellor at Law, at the time of Committing the felony and Murder aforesaid feloniously Wilfully and of their Malice aforethought ware present, abetting aiding assisting Comforting and Maintaining the said Aaron Burr to kill and Murder the Said Alexander Hamilton in Manner aforesaid. And So the Jurors aforesaid upon their Oath aforesaid do say the Said Aaron Burr and the Said William P Van Ness and Nathaniel Pendleton him the said Alexander Hamilton in Manner and by the means aforesaid, feloniously wilfully and of their Malice aforethought did kill and Murder, against the peace of the People of the State of New York and their Dignity.

In Witness Whereof as Well the aforesaid Coroner as the Jurors aforesaid have to this Inquisition put their seals on the Second day of August and in the year One thousand Eight hundred and four and at the place Aforesaid.

John Burger Coroner

> Alex^r Anderson
> Geo. Minuse
> John A Hardenbrook
> Peter Bonnett
> Elam Williams
> John Coffin
> John Mildeberger
> David A Brower
> David Lydig
> Ab^m. Bloodgood
> James Cummings
> Amos Curtis
> Isaac Burr
> Benj. Strong
> J D Miller

Dr. David Hosack to William Coleman[1]

[New York] August 17th, 1804.

Dear Sir,

To comply with your request is a painful task; but I will repress my feelings while I endeavour to furnish you with an enumeration of such particulars relative to the melancholy end of our beloved friend Hamilton, as dwell most forcibly on my recollection.

When called to him, upon his receiving the fatal wound, I found him half sitting on the ground, supported in the arms of Mr. Pendleton. His countenance of death I shall never forget — He had at that instant just strength to say, "This is a mortal wound, Doctor;" when he sunk away, and became to all appearance lifeless. I immediately stripped up his clothes, and soon, alas! ascertained that the direction of the ball must have been through some vital part.* His pulses were not to be felt; his respiration was entirely suspended; and

* For the satisfaction of some of General Hamilton's friends I examined his body after death, in presence of Dr. Post and two other gentlemen. I discovered that the ball struck the second or third false rib, fractured it about in the middle; it then passed through the liver and diaphragm, and, as nearly as we could ascertain without a minute examination, lodged in the first or second lumbar vertebra. The vertebra in which it was lodged was considerably splintered, so that the spiculae were distinctly perceptible to the finger. About a pint of clotted blood was found in the cavity of the belly, which had probably been effused from the divided vessels of the liver.

upon laying my hand on his heart, and perceiving no motion there, I considered him as irrecoverably gone. I however observed to Mr. Pendleton, that the only chance for his reviving was immediately to get him upon the water. We therefore lifted him up, and carried him out of the wood, to the margin of the bank, where the bargemen aided us in conveying him into the boat, which immediately put off. During all this time I could not discover the least symptom of returning life. I now rubbed his face, lips, and temples, with spirits of hartshorne, applied it to his neck and breast, and to the wrists and palms of his hands, and endeavoured to pour some into his mouth. When we had got, as I should judge, about 50 yards from the shore, some imperfect efforts to breathe were for the first time manifest: in a few minutes he sighed, and became sensible to the impression of the hartshorne, or the fresh air of the water: He breathed; his eyes, hardly opened, wandered, without fixing upon any objects; to our great joy he at length spoke: "My vision is indistinct," were his first words. His pulse became more perceptible; his respiration more regular; his sight returned. I then examined the wound to know if there was any dangerous discharge of blood; upon slightly pressing his side it gave him pain; on which I desisted. Soon after recovering his sight, he happened to cast his eye upon the case of pistols, and observing the one that he had had in his hand lying on the outside, he said,

1. William Coleman, ed., *A Collection of the Facts and Documents Relative to the Death of Major-General Alexander Hamilton* ... (New York, 1804), 18–22.

"Take care of that pistol; it is undischarged, and still cocked; it may go off and do harm; — Pendleton knows, (attempting to turn his head towards him) that I did not intend to fire at him." "Yes," said Mr. Pendleton, understanding his wish, "I have already made Dr. Hosack acquainted with your determination as to that." He then closed his eyes, and remained calm, without any disposition to speak; nor did he say much afterwards, excepting in reply to my questions as to his feelings. He asked me once or twice, how I found his pulse; and he informed me that his lower extremities had lost all feeling; manifesting to me that he entertained no hopes that he should long survive. I changed the posture of his limbs, but to no purpose; they had totally lost their sensibility. Perceiving that we approached the shore, he said, "Let Mrs. Hamilton be immediately sent for — let the event be gradually broken to her; but give her hopes." Looking up we saw his friend Mr. Bayard standing on the wharf in great agitation. He had been told by his servant that Gen. Hamilton, Mr. Pendleton, and myself, had crossed the river in a boat together, and too well he conjectured the fatal errand, and foreboded the dreadful result. Perceiving, as we came nearer, that Mr. Pendleton and myself only sat up in the stern sheets, he clasped his hands together in the most violent apprehension; but when I called to him to have a cot prepared, and he at the same moment saw his poor friend lying in the bottom of the boat, he threw up his eyes and burst into a flood of tears and lamentation. Hamilton alone appeared tranquil and composed. We then conveyed him as tenderly as possible up to the house. The distresses of this amiable family were such that till the first shock was abated, they were scarcely able to summon fortitude enough to yield sufficient assistance to their dying friend.

Upon our reaching the house he became more languid, occasioned probably by the agitation of his removal from the boat. I gave him a little weak wine and water. When he recovered his feelings, he complained of pain in his back; we immediately undressed him, laid him in bed, and darkened the room. I then gave him a large anodyne, which I frequently repeated. During the first day he took upwards of an ounce of laudanum; and tepid anodyne fomentations were also applied to those parts nearest the seat of his pain — Yet were his sufferings, during the whole of the day, almost intolerable.* I had not the shadow of a hope of his recovery, and Dr. Post,[2] whom I requested might be sent for immediately on our reaching Mr. Bayard's house, united with me in this opinion. General Rey,[3] the French Consul, also had the goodness

* As his habit was delicate and had been lately rendered more feeble by ill health, particularly by a disorder of the stomach and bowels, I carefully avoided all those remedies which are usually indicated on such occasions.

_____

2. Wright Post was a prominent New York physician and a member of the medical department of Columbia College.

3. Antoine-Venance Gabriel Rey, commissary of commercial relations in New York City.

to invite the surgeons of the French frigates in our harbour, as they had had much experience in gunshot wounds, to render their assistance. They immediately came; but to prevent his being disturbed I stated to them his situation, described the nature of his wound and the direction of the ball, with all the symptoms that could enable them to form an opinion as to the event. One of the gentlemen then accompanied me to bed side. The result was a confirmation of the opinion that had already been expressed by Dr. Post and myself.

During the night, he had some imperfect sleep; but the succeeding morning his symptoms were aggravated, attended however with a diminution of pain. His mind retained all its usual strength and composure. The great source of his anxiety seemed to be in his sympathy with his half distracted wife and children. He spoke to me frequently of them — "My beloved wife and children," were always his expressions. But his fortitude triumphed over his situation, dreadful as it was; once, indeed, at the sight of his children brought to the bed-side together, seven in number, his utterance forsook him; he opened his eyes, gave them one look, and closed them again, till they were taken away. As a proof of his extraordinary composure of mind, let me add, that he alone could calm the frantic grief of their mother. *"Remember, my Eliza, you are a Christian,"* were the expressions with which he frequently, with a firm voice, but in a pathetic and impressive manner, addressed her. His words, and the tone in which they were uttered, will never be effaced from my memory. At about two o'clock, as the public well knows, he expired.

> "Incorrupta fides — nudaque veritas
> Quando ullum invenient parem?
> Multis ille quidem flebilis occidit."

I am, Sir,
Your friend and humble serv't,
DAVID HOSACK

Wm. Coleman, Esq.

Statement of Dr. David Hosack's Services to Alexander Hamilton[1]

[New York, August 8, 1805]

The Estate of General Hamilton

                    To D Hosack   D^r

1804   To med and adv in January — February
               — March — May and June $37.50
               To attendance &c during his
               last illness   50

                                $87.50

                 Rec^d payment

New York Augt. 8th. 1805

                       D Hosack

1. DS, New-York Historical Society.

Interview in Weehawken

CONCLUSION

Conclusion

Hamilton's death, thirty-one hours after his wound, shocked the nation. Momentarily forgotten was the antagonism that many had felt toward him. To many Republicans who had long hated him as well as to many Federalists who were impatient to see his influence removed from their party — and of course to those people who loved and respected him regardless of party — he was suddenly a hero, even a martyr, sacrificed to the inveterate malice of the Vice-President of the United States. The solemn funeral ceremonies, at which Gouverneur Morris delivered an address tempered by moderation, were but the beginning of a period of mourning throughout the country.

Yet while press, pulpit, politicians, and people from all ranks of society showered eulogistic sentiments on the one principal, they hurled maledictions at the other. The coroner's jury in New York, with no jurisdiction in New Jersey where the duel occurred, reproved Burr and charged him with murder. Warned of the rising tide of emotion, he had already left for Perth Amboy, New Jersey, where he stayed at Commodore Truxton's, then went on to Philadelphia. Not long after arriving, he learned that New Jersey had also issued a murder indictment. He now rode to the South to let the situation cool off.

The death of Hamilton had a number of interesting repercussions. Although it raised hopes among Federalists that they might ride back into power on a wave of popular revulsion at the Republicans, people generally seemed to be able to distinguish Burr from his party as an object on which to vent their sense of outrage. The death, however, temporarily checked the New England secessionist movement among the Federalists by making Burr, who had been so important in their calculations and who had been defeated in New

York, *persona non grata* throughout the country. The death also reminded the nation that, however constant a storm center Hamilton had been, a great man had died — one whose powerful, incisive mind had made significant contributions to the new republic. In the American political hagiology he was at once deservedly accorded a high place — higher in 1804, perhaps, than it would have been if he had lived on, as did Burr, into the period of Jacksonian democracy. The Jacksonians would probably have been less tolerant than the Jeffersonians of a man whose conservatism had led him to admire the monarchy of George the Third and to deplore democracy, a man who could consider the Constitution as late as 1802 a "frail and worthless fabric" and could feel that "this American world was not made for me."[1] Heartless though it seems to say so, it may well be that for his apotheosis Alexander Hamilton died at the right time — possibly even a little late; but the ill effect of any such tardiness was obliterated by the manner of his death.

The condemnation of Burr was so sweeping that it raises the possibility of its having been partially contrived. Certainly the fierce denunciation by DeWitt Clinton and his supporters suggests that they were aware of the magnificent opportunity to discredit Burr completely and eventually to capture control of the Burrite faction. That Clinton himself was no stranger to the field of honor mattered not at all. In point of fact, the thirst for vengeance was so consuming that some thoughtful people became disturbed. Even Morgan Lewis, the Republican Governor of New York and no friend to Burr, was reported to have denounced the proceedings of the coroner's jury and the haste to issue an illegal murder indictment as "disgraceful, illiberal and ungentlemanly."[2] A friend of Hamilton, Judge Richard Peters of Pennsylvania, said of the duel, "As an old military man Colonel Burr could not have acted otherwise than he did. I never knew Colonel Burr [to] speak ill of any man, and he had a right to expect a different treatment from what he experienced."[3] Gouverneur Morris, who at times had worked closely with Hamilton, said that "Colonel Burr ought to be considered in the same light with any other man who had killed another in a duel."[4] John Randolph of Virginia, perhaps reflecting the easier attitude of the South and West toward dueling, declared that Burr's conduct in the Hamilton affair "does him honor."[5]

Indeed Randolph's appraisal was very acute. He said of the duel correspondence, which Professor Syrett and Mrs. Cooke have presented in this volume:[6] "How visible is his [Burr's] ascendancy over him [Hamilton], and how sensible does the latter appear of it! There is an apparent consciousness of some inferiority to his enemy displayed by Hamilton throughout that transaction, and, from a previous sight of their letters, I could have inferred the issue of the contest. On one side, there is labored obscurity, much equivocation, and many attempts at evasion, not unmixed with a little blustering; on the other an unshaken adherence to his object, and an undeviating pursuit of it not to be eluded or baffled. It reminded me of a sinking fox, pressed by a vigorous old hound, where no shift is permitted to avail him."[7]

Such is the impression that the letters give to anyone reading them today, after a lapse of a century and a half. Had Hamilton declared outright that he had uttered nothing that could be described as "a still more despicable opinion" — at least nothing that applied to Burr's private character — the altercation might have come to an abrupt stop. Instead, he demanded a bill of particulars, a move that placed him in Burr's hands. From this point on, as letters passed quickly back and forth, Burr kept pressing for an explanation, while Hamilton strove with anguish and unavailing circumlocutions to maintain his dignity and at the same time to placate Burr. But he could not satisfy his rival. Perhaps, indeed, Burr would have been satisfied with no explanation. Hamilton had earlier expressed the belief that Burr would be the instrument of his death, and Burr certainly conducted himself in the correspondence as if he were truly fated for the role of executioner. On the other hand, Burr was quite within his rights under the code duello in demanding an explanation, and it can hardly be said that Hamilton's attempts to explain were frank and convincing.

One may wonder, of course, why Hamilton did not refuse the challenge, why he did not scorn it or laugh at it. He did not approve of dueling, or so he said: private combat was forbidden by law, and besides, it was contrary to his religious and moral principles. But he himself had challenged before, and he had lost his oldest son to Eacker's pistol. Moreover, he was a man of his generation, with an important position in the public eye; and in his generation, dueling was a widely accepted agency by which personal honor was maintained. Hence, the circumstances of the crisis being what they were, he could scarcely have avoided accepting the challenge.

The more so because he knew that Burr was right. In the statement opened after his death, he frankly conceded that "my animadversions on the political principles character and views of Col Burr have been extremely severe, and on different occasions I, in common with many others, have made very unfavourable criticisms on particular instances of the private conduct of this Gentleman." He thought he might have injured Burr; hence he would meet him, would even throw away his first fire. Besides, in Hamilton's view, there existed "a peculiar necessity not to decline the call." "The ability to be in future useful," he explained, "whether in resisting mischief or in effecting good, in those crises in our public affairs, which seem likely to happen, would probably be inseparable from a conformity with public prejudice in this particular."[8] He did not seem to realize fully that his political career and influence, as well as Burr's, were already ruined, perhaps beyond repair; but even that realization would probably not have altered his decision.

By the same token, Burr could not permit the insulting treatment to which he had been exposed by DeWitt Clinton and Hamilton to pass without objection. Clinton had done his work largely through the newspaper editor Cheetham, who as a journalist was beneath a gentleman's notice except possibly for a lawsuit or a horsewhipping. Hamilton also had used the press; but beyond that, his name was directly and inextricably linked with personal aspersion, thanks to the publication of Cooper's letters. Moreover, he had been Burr's rival for many years; like Burr, he had been prominent in the nation's affairs since the Revolution and had held high national office; and he was leader of the opposition political party, not merely of a dissident faction. Burr chose him rather than Clinton as the more suitable and more obvious opponent.

So the deed was done; and Burr never succeeded in moving out of the shadow of that tragic day. After a time he returned to chair the Senate, where he presided with great skill and dignity at the impeachment trial of Justice Samuel Chase, and then took leave of his colleagues in an eloquent speech that reduced many of them to tears. The West fascinated him, and he made an extended trip through it. Returning to Washington, he made plans for buying a half-million acres in the newly acquired Louisiana territory and establishing a colony there. It was alleged, however, that he also planned to lead the then Southwest against

Mexico and even to form a new nation partially from territory that belonged to the United States. Betrayed by one of his fellow conspirators, the tarnished warrior General James Wilkinson, who was acting as a Spanish intelligence agent at the same time that he commanded the American military forces in the Southwest, Burr was brought to Richmond in 1807 for one of the most celebrated treason trials in American legal history. The legal contest was as much a political and judicial struggle between Republican President Jefferson in Washington and Federalist Chief Justice John Marshall in Richmond as it was a case of the United States versus Aaron Burr. The accused was ultimately declared not guilty on the basis of the evidence submitted; this Scotch verdict by the jury was indicative of the suspicion with which Burr was generally regarded. For that matter the Burr conspiracy, elaborate and complex, still remains a subject of scholarly investigation, with the judgments increasingly pointing to a treasonous involvement on Burr's part.[9]

Burr now went to Europe, where he traveled extensively from 1808 to 1812. Desperate for funds, he borrowed money which he could not hope to repay, at least for a long time, often lived on the largesse of friends and acquaintances, and not infrequently won sums at the card table. He met many of the political and literary great men of that exciting era, including the English social philosopher Jeremy Bentham — who, for all his fondness for Burr, is alleged to have considered the duel with Hamilton as "little better than a murder."[10]

Back in New York by mid–1812, Burr faced another kind of tragedy. He learned that Theodosia's son, Aaron Burr Alston, whom he loved dearly and who he hoped would one day vindicate him, had died of disease. Theodosia herself, his beloved and talented daughter, was so grief-stricken and ill that he sent for

174

her to come to New York. To his horror, the ship on which she sailed was first stopped by a British man-of-war, then utterly disappeared — presumably in a storm, although for years there lingered rumors of pirates and wreckers. From this double loss Burr seems never to have completely recovered.

He lived until 1836, making a living of sorts as an attorney, having numerous affairs, marrying and then quickly separating from a wealthy widow of questionable reputation, who was as wretched with him as he with her and whose divorce decree was issued on the day he died. Although often ill and short of funds, Burr continued to the end elegant in manners and careful in dress. But people often remarked about his large dark eyes, which had always been very penetrating. Some thought they saw sadness in them; others, madness. "What I remember most vividly were his terrible eyes," was one comment.[11] They blazed with excitement one day when he read in a newspaper that an adventurous crowd of Americans had been responsible for declaring Texas independent of Mexico. "*There!* you see? I was right!" he exclaimed to a friend. "I was only thirty years too soon! What was treason in me thirty years ago, is patriotism now!!"[12] On another day his eyes must have looked strange indeed when, reading Lawrence Sterne's *Tristram Shandy,* a favorite with him, he came to the passage where Uncle Toby carefully puts the fly out of the window with the observation that the world is wide enough for them both. "If I had read Sterne more, and Voltaire less," Burr said to the young man visiting him, "I should have known that the world was wide enough for Hamilton and me."[13]

One might have thought that the Hamilton-Burr duel would have put an end to dueling in the United States. Although it certainly increased popular aversion to the practice, it brought no end to meetings on the field of honor. Two such engagements enjoyed a special notoriety. One occurred in 1820 when the dashing naval hero Commodore Stephen Decatur fell before the pistol of a fellow officer, Captain James Barron, who in 1807 had surrendered the *Chesapeake* to H.M.S. *Leopard* without clearing for action, who had been suspended from command in consequence, and whose application for restoration to active duty Decatur had opposed. The second occurred in 1838 when the brilliant Congressman Jonathan Cilley of Maine was shot and killed by Congressman William J. Graves of Kentucky. The circumstances of this duel were peculiarly affecting, for the two men esteemed each other and the original difference of opinion had existed between Cilley and Colonel James Watson Webb, whose note to Cilley, borne by Graves, the Maine congressman had refused to receive. As Webb's representative, Graves himself had then promptly challenged Cilley — a procedure strictly according to the code duello. Cilley had accepted to avoid disgrace.

Whereas the Burr-Hamilton duel, as well as that between Decatur and Barron, had inspired chiefly expressions of regret and condemnation of both the victor and the practice of personal combat, the Cilley-Graves duel stirred up some action. A shocked Congress outlawed the giving or accepting of a challenge to fight a duel in the District of Columbia. States too had their laws, but dueling with swords, pistols, and even rifles continued for years. It was not until after the Civil War that dueling generally went out of fashion and began to be popularly regarded not so much as dishonorable or barbarous, not to mention illegal, but as absurd in a modern industrial society. The change in attitude may account in some small part for the increase in suits for libel and slander during the late nineteenth century. An offended person now looked to his lawyer instead of his pistol.

Yet in the wide open areas of the cattle-raising and mining West, where gunmen fought it out with each other or with hard-faced sheriffs and marshals, remnants of the old code — probably never recognized as such — persisted. The only "honorable" combat was with pistols or rifles (never fists!), while to shoot an unarmed man at any time or even an armed officer of the law when his back was turned was hardly "cricket" even with this lawless clan, though both were sometimes done.

Now even such vulgar remnants of the code duello are long since gone. All that remains is a memory of action between high-spirited gentlemen — and the imagination catches the flash of the morning sun on a rapier blade or the whiff of pistol smoke. In the context of American history, that memory is usually focused on the famous and tragic meeting on the banks of the Hudson.

Notes

1. Hamilton to Gouverneur Morris, February 27, 1802. Hamilton Papers, Library of Congress.

2. John Swartwout to Burr, August 2, 1804. Davis, *Memoirs of Aaron Burr,* II, 329.

3. Charles Biddle, *Autobiography* (Philadelphia, 1883), 303.

4. *The Diary and Letters of Gouverneur Morris,* edited by Anne C. Morris (2 vols., New York, 1888), II, 457–458.

5. William Cabell Bruce, *John Randolph of Roanoke* (2 vols. in one, New York, 1922), I, 298.

6. The previous collection generally used has been the incomplete and comparatively unannotated edition published by William Coleman in New York, 1804, and

reprinted in 1904: *A Collection of the Facts and Documents relative to the Death of Major-General Hamilton; with Comments: Together with the various Orations, Sermons, and Eulogies, that have been Published or Written on his Life and Character.*

7. Quoted in Bruce, *op. cit.*, I, 298.

8. "Alexander Hamilton's Remarks on his Impending Duel with Aaron Burr." See pages 98–102.

9. The most recent full-length study — and an excellent piece of scholarship — is Thomas Perkins Abernethy, *The Burr Conspiracy* (New York, 1954). An earlier study, somewhat more favorable to Burr, is Walter Flavius McCaleb, *The Aaron Burr Conspiracy* (New York, 1903). For the trial in particular, see also Francis F. Beirne, *Shout Treason: The Trial of Aaron Burr* (New York, 1959).

10. Lorenzo Sabine, *Notes on Duels and Duelling* (Boston, 1859), 212.

11. William Cary Duncan, *The Amazing Madame Jumel* (New York, 1935), 262.

12. Parton, *op. cit.*, 670.

13. *Ibid.*, 672–673.

Interview in Weehawken

has been composed in Linotype Baskerville, a faithful recutting of the celebrated types designed in the 1750's by John Baskerville. Though not widely used in America at the time, Baskerville's types were warmly championed by Benjamin Franklin and clearly influenced later American type design.

Composed and printed by Connecticut Printers, Inc., Hartford. The illustrations have been printed by offset lithography by the Meriden Gravure Company, Meriden, Connecticut. Bound by the Vail-Ballou Press, Binghamton, New York.

WESLEYAN UNIVERSITY PRESS
MIDDLETOWN, CONNECTICUT